DANVILLE

DANVILLE

• Heart of the San Ramon Valley •

Beverly Lane

The History PRESS

Published by The History Press
An imprint of Arcadia Publishing
Charleston, SC
www.historypress.com

Joe and Elizabeth Foster in front of the Danville Emporium, circa 1914. *Museum of the San Ramon Valley.*
View of Wood Ranch and Mount Diablo, circa 1974. *Wood family archives.*

First published 2026

Manufactured in the United States

ISBN 9781467156783

Library of Congress Control Number: 2025944853

CONTENTS

ACKNOWLEDGEMENTS

Many people helped create this book about the heart of the San Ramon Valley, Danville.

Jeff Mason, who made possible the inclusion of a number of the images and took photographs himself, deserves special recognition and my eternal thanks. Others who helped find, process, and provide new images include Cynthia Wood Rivera, Chuck Fereira, Vickie Sciacca, Newell Arnerich, Bob Sada, Fred Korbmacher, Joe Calabrigo, Jenn Starnes, the Danville Area Chamber of Commerce, Brian Doss, and Brian McElvoy.

Historical accounts of Danville have appeared in numerous books and articles, beginning with the detailed *History of Contra Costa*, written in 1882 by J.P. Munro-Fraser. Professor James Smith's remarkable memories about the 1850s and 1860s were invaluable; they appeared in several newspapers as "Looking Back to the Days When the Gringo First Came" and in a book titled *Recollections.*

Irma M. Dotson's extraordinary books on Downtown Danville, the Southern Pacific Railroad, and the Oakland, Antioch, and Eastern Railway have been used throughout this book. Other writers, past and present, provided local information and helpful insights; they include Ross Smith, Joe Calabrigo, Virgie V. Jones, Robert D. Tatum, Charlotte Wood, Juan Crespi, R.O. Baldwin, Allie Goold, Inez Butz, Fay Tarlock, Robert Burgess, Ralph Cozine, Richard Rutherford, Vivian Coats Edmonston, Wendy Cooper, Viola Root, Don Wood, Wilson Close, Randall Milliken, Arnold Blackmur, Rose Peters Emery, John Mercurio, and Steve Minnear.

Archives from the Bancroft Library, Museum of the San Ramon Valley, and Contra Costa County Historical Society's History Center were used and much appreciated. Newspaper articles from the *Contra Costa Gazette* and the *Valley Pioneer* informed much of the manuscript as well.

Vivienne Wong, Alice Chambliss, Joe Calabrigo, and Wendy Cooper read all or parts of this book, for which I am extremely grateful. In addition, conversations or interviews with these individuals, past and present, deserve credit: Chuck Fereira, Gary Soto, Sharon Burke, Rose Ferreira, Fritz Ferreira, Millie Freitas, Kathryn Benvenuto, Donna Grier, Joe Calabrigo, Jan Berckefeldt, Ginny Fereira, David Crompton, Betty Dunlap, Renee Morgan, Roanne Ross, Newell Arnerich, Karen Stepper, Robert Storer, Mark Belotz, Doug Offenhartz, Fred Korbmacher Henry Perezalonso, Shari Gonzalez and Don Wood. I'm also appreciative of the Museum of San Ramon Valley staff members Dan Dunn and Jamie Ingrassia for their support.

Thanks to you all. Finally, my gratitude goes to my son Doug Lane, who facilitated many history projects at the Museum of the San Ramon Valley and who urged me to complete this book on Danville.

INTRODUCTION

Danville's history reflects California's, beginning with the Native people, the Spanish invasion and the Gold Rush. In this fertile valley, the early pioneers managed farms and ranches for a century. They built schools and churches, founded the Danville Grange No. 85, and created a community in an ideal setting. When the San Ramon Branch Line of the Southern Pacific opened in 1891, the small hamlet grew to become the heart of the San Ramon Valley.

Danville is unique in part because the groundbreaking playwright Eugene O'Neill lived in the western hills from 1937 to 1944. In the serenity of his "final home and harbor" at Tao House, he wrote his last great plays, including *Long Day's Journey into Night* and *The Iceman Cometh*.

Boosters often praised the advantages of living in Danville. One example came from the *Contra Costa Courier and Danville Journal* on March 12, 1914:

> *Never did the San Ramon Valley present a more attractive appearance than now, and in the past it has always been pronounced one of the most beautiful spots of earth. The balmy spring air is laden with the perfume of thousands of fruit blossoms and the green hills with the growing grain in the rich valley are delightful to look on.*

Three books about Danville have previously been published, *Danville: A Portrait of 125 Years* (1985), *Downtown Danville 1976–2001* (2001) and *Vintage*

Danville, 150 Years of Memories (2008). This book—with new pictures and information from Danville's past—is designed to tell new and old stories about the area's settlers; the freeway's impact on development; the town's beginning in 1982; and life in the twenty-first century.

1
A CENTENNIAL TO REMEMBER

Danville had a splashy party in 1958 to celebrate its centennial. With World War II behind them, a growing population and an interstate freeway in their future, Danville residents were eager to produce a festive occasion and recognize the town's historic founding in 1858. The population had grown from 1,225 in 1940 to 9,809 in 1957.

Danville Began with the Inman Brothers

Dan Inman and his brother Andrew came to California beset with gold fever, along with thousands of others from the East Coast, Europe and across the Pacific. The Inmans traveled from Illinois to the gold country in 1849.

Panning for gold was rough, but since the brothers came soon after the 1848 gold discovery, they made some money. In late 1849, the Inmans bought a boardinghouse in Sacramento, only to have winter floods ruin the property. Returning to the mines, they worked around Hangtown, Grass Valley, and other locations. In 1852, the brothers came to a beautiful area southwest of Mount Diablo called Green Valley to raise cattle and sheep. Andrew married Ann Young and settled in. But not Dan.

In 1854, Dan and a good friend Jesse Bowles tried (and failed) to grow tobacco on thirty acres south of Danville. Then Dan went back and forth from Green Valley to mining country. He made his stake in El Dorado, using a new and profitable technique called hydraulic mining.

Dan and Josephine Jones Inman. Dan's property became the village of Danville in 1858. *Museum of the San Ramon Valley.*

Forty years later, Inman wrote an account of his final return in the January 1898 *Danville Sentinel*:

> *I reached Danville, or the site where it now stands, in June 1852. I spent the summer in the valley but returned to the mines in the fall. In the summer of 1853 I came into the valley again and remained until 1857, when I returned to the mines. In March of the following year (1858) I came into the valley once more—this time for good—and purchased a farm, where Danville is now located, of a man named Pigmore. I went to farming and seeded the lands with wheat that winter.*
>
> *In the summer of 1859 a man named Davis came along and wanted to start a blacksmith shop where the one now stands (Close's) and I gave him permission to do so. He sold out that winter to Jim Johnson, now deceased. Johnson soon after sold to Simon Whitmore.*
>
> *Then a man named Long started a wheelwright shop. About the same time H.W. Harris started a hotel and Wolff & Cohen a storer.*
>
> *Then the people of the valley wanted a post office. Of course it had to have a name, and quite a number were suggested. At first they thought of calling it Inmanville, but my brother Andrew and I objected to that.*

> *Finally, Grandma Young, my brother's mother-in-law, said "Call it Danville," and, as much or more out of respect for her, as she was born and raised near Danville, Kentucky, it took that name.*

The property Inman purchased was located at the intersection of Tassajara Road and Front Street on both sides of San Ramon Creek. It turned out to be an ideal location for businesses, and the village began—like many other pioneer towns—with a blacksmith, hotel, general store, and wheelwright. In 1860, a post office was established in the Danville Hotel, with owner Henry Harris as postmaster.

A trained cooper himself, Inman continued farming and eventually opened his own carriage-making shop. In 1863, he married Josephine Jones, a daughter of Alamo founders Mary Ann and John Jones, when he was thirty-six and she was sixteen. Later, they moved to Livermore, where he became an Alameda County supervisor, the first Livermore Grange worthy master, and a delegate to the 1878 California Constitutional Convention. The couple had seven children.

The Next Century

Fast-forward one hundred years. In the 1950s, Danville had ranches and orchards that spread out from town and small businesses lining its main street, Hartz Avenue. But there were also many gas stations, lots of frayed-looking business fronts, and an unpleasantly steady stream of cars on State Route 21 through town. Freeway rights-of-way were purchased, and meetings about the future alignment were well attended. In 1964, traffic would bypass the town when the I-680 Freeway opened from Walnut Creek to Sycamore Valley Road.

Downtown merchants took a good look at the area, which had been nicknamed "Gasoline Alley," and decided to make some changes. In 1952, livewire promotor Russel Glenn restored the Danville Hotel and built a ghost town–inspired patio with Western-themed store fronts, all with an eye to draw visitors to the community.

He touted a "planned retrogression" to improve Danville's image. John May, Semmes Gordon, John Roberts, and Dr. Tom Ohlson joined Glenn to create the "Confederacy of Danville." The Lions, Danville Rotary, and Business and Professional Women joined the project in support. It was likely

A Danville Confederacy wagon and sign placed at the south end of town. *Left to right*: Tony Cicero, John May, and Bill Hockins. *Museum of the San Ramon Valley.*

the leaders had a good time planning all of this, probably fueled by some after-work get-togethers and adult libations.

They encouraged merchants to spiff up their business in a western style, plant more trees, and put flowers in planter boxes. Chamber of commerce President Ohlson placed a bathtub with flowers outside his veterinary business on Rose Street, while May's Shoe Stable already looked traditional. The Confederacy of Danville passed a "Declaration of Independence of Danville 1958," which declared that they "hereby withdraw from the twentieth century.…We propose, God willing, to form a Confederation and to rebuild our town completely as it was in 1858 as an oasis of peace and tranquility for other Americans to visit."

The Confederacy's theme was "Old Century Leisure, New Century Convenience." A display of drawings by artist Alfred Ahronian toured the town, touting the new "old" look. Danville's declaration was featured in newspapers beyond the Bay Area. Glenn even purchased a billboard in San Francisco, which asked, "Where the Hell is Danville?" Then he provided an answer on his 1965 Silver Dollar Saloon napkins, edited here:

Where the Hell Is Danville?

In almost the center of the greenest, prettiest, most peaceful valley in the world!

Free from smog, city traffic, industrial activity and other by-products of metropolitan centers, she enjoys the proximity of the big cities while maintaining a country aloofness.

One can drive from the choked, smoke-filled streets of San Francisco, and in less than a half hour, be riding along a narrow, bucolic country road, replete with grazing cattle, rustic farmhouses and tired windmills…a century away from the city grind.

Where is Danville? You might say it's smack in the middle of tranquil living…where the pursuit of happiness and concern for one's fellow man are still in style…where one can stretch without feeling hemmed in, or can ride a horse, walk a dog, peddle a bike…or anything else he wants to do… in a relaxed, secure uncrowded environment.

THAT'S where it's at.

The Centennial Hay Days Celebration

What better way to draw attention to the "newly old" Danville than to have a celebration? Inman's land purchase could be dated to 1858, so a huge centennial party was planned for 1958. The *Valley Pioneer*'s publisher, Semmes Gordon, produced a centennial edition on September 4, which featured a congratulatory telegram from President Dwight Eisenhower.

Four days of celebrations marked the occasion from September 4 to September 7, with Charlotte Wood School serving as the event's main site. There was an aquacade, an old-timers bathing suit fashion show, a carnival, a kid's day, and a pet parade, along with the Danville Junior Horsemen's show at the Humphrey arena, the coronation of Miss Pioneer Belle, a dance, a flag-raising ceremony, and barbecued steak community dinner. A beard-growing contest received mixed reviews. The Hay Days Parade featured native son Congressman John F. Baldwin Jr., marching bands, pioneer descendants in wagons, horse units, and much flag-waving.

The *Valley Pioneer*'s centennial edition provided long histories on the valley's agriculture, schools, Natives, and Mount Diablo, plus sketches of nineteenth-century pioneers. One article pointed out that Danville had twenty-one namesakes in the country.

Above: The centennial parade in Danville, with Congressman John F. Baldwin Jr. (without a hat). *Museum of the San Ramon Valley.*

Right: A portrait of Charlotte Wood, circa 1900. She taught at Sycamore Grammar School for thirty-one years and was the Grange poet, a historian, and a party giver whom everyone called "Aunt Lottie." *Wood family archives.*

Fay Tarlock wrote "Danville—A Portrait," which provided a history of the area from the Gold Rush to the suburbs. She noted that downtown Danville was clustered around Hartz Avenue, with walnut orchards surrounding the village until the late 1950s.

Finally, teacher and Grange poet laureate ninety-four-year-old Charlotte Wood produced one of her poems for the occasion, edited here:

Our Danville

To our olden-time Danville and the years long passed by,
We would turn in true reverence, with fond memory and tender sigh,
For those brave sturdy builders of the pioneer days,
Are with us no longer save in history's maze.

They came filled with vigor, with enthusiasm and cheer
Buoyed with hope, inspiration—never daunted by fear;
Through their wisdom, their courage, their labor and zeal
We, of today, have gained from their hard-earned weal.

What spot more enchanting, more inviting, more fine,
Than this beautiful valley rich in verdure and vine?
Wild oats waving gently in the soft western breeze,
The brook's winding course outlined by its myriad trees.

The hill-slopes near by with golden poppies aglow—
Wild paint-brush, brodeia, baby-blue-eyes, and so
To this primeval valley, Mt. Diablo its guard,
Came these pioneer people to Nature's garden, unmarred.

Many Churches and Clubs have come on apace
Bringing new interests, new Shops, new duties to face.
Now we'll enjoy the new beauty with the colorful trees
Which add to the comfort and the fragrance of each wanton breeze.

Then All Hail to Our Danville on this "Centennial Year"!
May a wealth of rich blessings crown each twelve-month so dear
And Peace reign triumphant; Peace and Good Cheer!

2
DANVILLE'S SETTING AND FIRST PEOPLE

From its beginnings, Danville has experienced a history of change and growth in an ideal setting. Founded around San Ramon Creek and framed by Mount Diablo and Las Trampas Ridge, Danville is known for its enviable quality of life. The beauty of the area and its mild weather have made it a desirable place to live for thousands of years, starting with the Native peoples.

An Intriguing Geology

Geologic forces and water have shaped the area in some unique ways. Like the rest of the San Francisco Bay area, the Danville region was once covered with water and evolved as the major Pacific and North American tectonic plates shifted over millions of years.

Mount Diablo, northeast of Danville, has an unusual geology. The core of the mountain is composed of an uplifted jumble of rocks from the Franciscan formation that was exposed by the erosion of overlying rocks from the Cretaceous and Miocene formations. A contemporary state park "Trail through Time" enables visitors to view the mountain's various geologic layers.

From 1862 to 1864, some copper was found and mined in veins in the diabase on the northwest side of Mount Diablo, with a small amount

A photograph of Mount Diablo, which, at 3,849 feet high, presides over San Francisco's East Bay. *Museum of the San Ramon Valley.*

A drawing of the valley's savanna and the gomphotheriums (predecessors of the mastodon), which lived in the valley thousands of years ago. *Artist, Carl Buell; Museum of the San Ramon Valley.*

produced. A century later, there were unsuccessful attempts to find oil or gas after substantial dredging in Las Trampas Hills. In 1963, the McCollough Oil Company erected rigs and drilled into an old sea bed, and the following year, Phillips Petroleum found some oil and natural gas but none in commercial quantities.

A quarry full of fossilized remains located to the east of Danville and south of the mountain has been explored by the University of California, Berkeley since the 1930s. The Blackhawk Quarry was discovered in 1936 by a graduate student Nestor John Sandor. Since then, over three thousand specimens have been unearthed and are now stored at the Museum of Paleontology on the University of California, Berkeley, campus. Mastodons, dire wolves, saber-toothed cats, three-toed horses, camels and plant fossils reveal what the area's life was like thousands of years ago.

EARTHQUAKE COUNTRY

As they have in the rest of California, earthquakes have jolted the Danville area. Tear faults travel southwest from Mount Diablo through Green Valley and across Diablo-Tassajara Road to San Ramon Creek. The northern part of the Calaveras Fault slices beneath the earth and is covered by ancient landslides that border Las Trampas Ridge. This ridge forms the hills west of Danville and Alamo and is a thrust-faulted anticlinal structure, underlain by a series of natural springs. *Calaveras* means "skulls" in Spanish.

A July 4, 1861 Calaveras shaker was reported, which broke out new streams in San Ramon and tumbled down the historic Amador two-story adobe in Dublin. It had an estimated magnitude of 6 on the Richter scale.

Substantial temblors on the Hayward Fault in 1868 and the San Andreas Fault in 1906 and 1989 some distance west of Danville produced local damage and are remembered in diaries and newspapers. One *Contra Costa Gazette* article in 1868 said:

> *So far as we have any record or tradition, the earthquake of Wednesday morning last was altogether the most violent and alarming that has occurred here since this portion of our coast has been known to civilized men.*

Cynthia Wood told her daughter Charlotte that during the 1868 quake, "the branches of the old oak swept the earth with its force; the stone milk house was wrecked…and chimneys turned halfway around." The Wood Ranch is located about seventeen miles from the Hayward Fault.

The 7.9 magnitude San Francisco earthquake and fire on April 18, 1906, destroyed 80 percent of the city and killed an estimated three thousand people. In Danville, the *Contra Costa Gazette*, on April 19, 1906, reported, "There is scarcely a chimney left throughout the valley and there were many narrow escapes but, so far as learned, no one was injured. Great excitement prevailed." Las Trampas Hills were lit up from the fire that followed.

The San Ramon Valley has the dubious distinction of being the Bay Area's center for earthquake swarms, defined as energetic sequences of small earthquakes occurring over a relatively short period. The Calaveras and the Mount Diablo Thrust Faults have produced six earthquake swarms in Danville and Alamo since 1970, ranging from two to forty-two days long. In 1990, a swarm lasted forty-two days, with the largest quake reaching a magnitude of 4.4; in 2018, another swarm provided sixty small temblors in a few days, with the largest measuring 3.6 on the Richter scale.

Registering an impressive magnitude of 6.9, the Loma Prieta earthquake on October 17, 1989, was the largest in recent decades. It occurred during the "Battle of the Bay," the World Series between the Oakland A's and the San Francisco Giants baseball teams. Millions of television viewers watched as sport commentators reported on the shaking baseball stadium and the Bay Bridge's partial collapse. Caused by a slip along the San Andreas Fault, the quake lasted ten to fifteen seconds and killed 63 people, injured 3,757 and left some 12,000 homeless throughout Northern California.

Wanting to help, Danville caterer Susan May Foord went to Diablo Foods, stepped around items on the floor, and brought home bread, peanut butter, and jelly. She made boxes of sandwiches for the firefighters in San Francisco. The next day, she and a friend drove over the Richmond–San Rafael and Golden Gate Bridges to reach the firefighters' staging area, where they were welcomed with open arms. News coverage that night mentioned the two Danville ladies who came to the rescue.

The Solitary Mountain

Mount Diablo emerges out of a relatively flat part of California, and the 3,849-foot peak can be seen from hundreds of miles away. On a clear day, summit visitors can view the Sierras, the Farallon Islands and Yosemite's

Partygoers celebrating a new Mount Diablo Park and Game Reserve on June 19, 1921. The park covered 630 acres and was one of seven state parks created before the California State Park system began in 1927. *Museum of the San Ramon Valley.*

Half Dome. Danville is located southwest of the iconic mountain. It was a sacred location for the region's Native peoples, who formed two dozen nations within a twenty-five-square-mile radius of the mountain.

The first recorded European name for the mountain was Cerro Alto de los Bolbones (High Point of the Volvons), a name that recognized the Bay Miwok–speaking Volvon Indians who lived north of the mountain. In 1805, a group of Bay Miwok Chupcans fled from Spanish troops in today's north Concord. Hearing strange sounds in the night and finding no Natives in the morning, the soldiers called the marsh Monte Del Diablo, or "Thicket of the Devil" in old Spanish. The name was later affixed to a rancho and the mountain.

The summit has the distinction of being an initial point for the U.S. Land Survey, the U.S. Coast and Geodetic Survey, and the 1860s Whitney Geological Survey. William H. Brewer, who worked on the Whitney Survey, also recorded new California flora, including Brewer's lupine, monkeyflower, and jewel flower, and described the tarantula spiders he saw as "a size that must be seen to be appreciated."

There are several accesses to today's Mount Diablo State Park, with the main access coming from the I-680 Freeway in Danville. The park is the linchpin for regional and city parks that surround the mountain and provides 120,000 acres of preserved open space. Mount Diablo is the northern point of the vast Diablo Range, which comprises 3.5 million acres extending 200 miles to the south.

People of the Land

For thousands of years, people lived in Danville, adjacent to creeks and springs nestled between Mount Diablo and Las Trampas Hills. They lived in villages with populations of twenty to two hundred at the time of Spanish contact. The Indians understood their area intimately, with an extensive knowledge of the region's plants and an awareness of its multiple sacred places. These Native people rarely traveled out of their homeland and supported extensive trade networks with other tribes.

At the time of non-Native contact, there were six Bay Miwok–speaking nations centered in Contra Costa County, located between Mount Diablo and the Carquinez Strait: Chupcan in Concord; Ompin in Bay Point; Julpun in East County; Saclan in Walnut Creek, Lafayette and points west; Volvon

A drawing of Bay Area Natives in 1816, showing them in feathered dance regalia. *Artist, Louis Choris; Bancroft Library.*

in Clayton and around the mountain; and Tatcan in San Ramon, Danville, and Alamo. Ohlone/Costanoan–speaking tribes lived south of Danville. Most Indigenous people spoke two or more languages.

The Danville Tatcans had a culture that changed very gradually and was sustained using multiple oral traditions. Their main village was probably adjacent to the creek where Old Town Danville is located. They followed seasonal rounds as they fished; gathered seeds and acorns; hunted rabbit, antelope, birds, and deer; and managed the land with fire and plant-pruning. Professor Lowell Bean stated that the tribal men were usually in charge of ceremonies and the sacred elements of Indian cosmology, while women managed the secular world. Respect for all aspects of the land was taught from childhood.

Festivals and gatherings in villages and on Mount Diablo often lasted for days and provided Native people an opportunity to relax, trade, meet new people, dance, and perform sacred rites. It was important to have a balanced world, and this was ensured by these dances and ceremonies. Ethnohistorian Randall Milliken wrote:

> *Throughout Central California, dances and their associated festivities were the main forms of communal religious expression. Dances were acts of veneration to natural and supernatural powers. It was believed that they helped maintain an undisturbed world order when properly carried out.*

Milliken added, "There are indications that the Chochenyo Ohlone, Coast Miwok and Bay Miwok participated in forms of the Kuksu Cult…which had secret dance societies and shared many elements of dance traditions."

Mount Diablo was a sacred place for all Native peoples within its viewshed. Beverly Ortiz wrote, "The remnant stories point to Mount Diablo as the creation point of the current physical world, the site where the leaders of the animal beings caused fog or water to fall away, and the land to appear." The top of the mountain had special meaning, and only sanctified shamans or priests could enter to perform rituals there. Seasonal camps were also established nearby, as can be seen with the many bedrock mortar holes at Rock City and other campgrounds.

Tribes named the mountain and had epic creation accounts set at Mount Diablo. An Ohlone name for the mountain was *Tuyshtak* and a northern Miwok name was *Oj-ompil-e*. The following is a fragment of one Native creation narrative from the Julpun, a Bay Miwok group:

> *Mol-luk (Condor Man) lived on the north side of Mount Diablo. His wife, the rock on which he roosted, gave birth to Wek-wek (Prairie-falcon Man). With the help of his grandfather Olette (Coyote Man), Wek-wek created Indian people, providing them with "everything everywhere so they can live."*
>
> *Wek-wek and Olette planted elderberry trees to provide music, food, and medicine for the people they were going to make. To create people, Wek-wek and Olette captured three bird beings and plucked their feathers. They traveled to places where they wanted villages and stuck three feathers in the ground. The feathers came to life and became people. Olette turned himself into a coyote and Wek-wek changed into a falcon.*

Contact with Spanish soldiers and missionaries in the 1700s led to the destruction of the Indian peoples' landscape and traditional society. Their seed meadows were destroyed by cattle and sheep, diseases for which they lacked immunity decimated them, and the powerful new ideas and weapons of the Spanish drew young people to the missions.

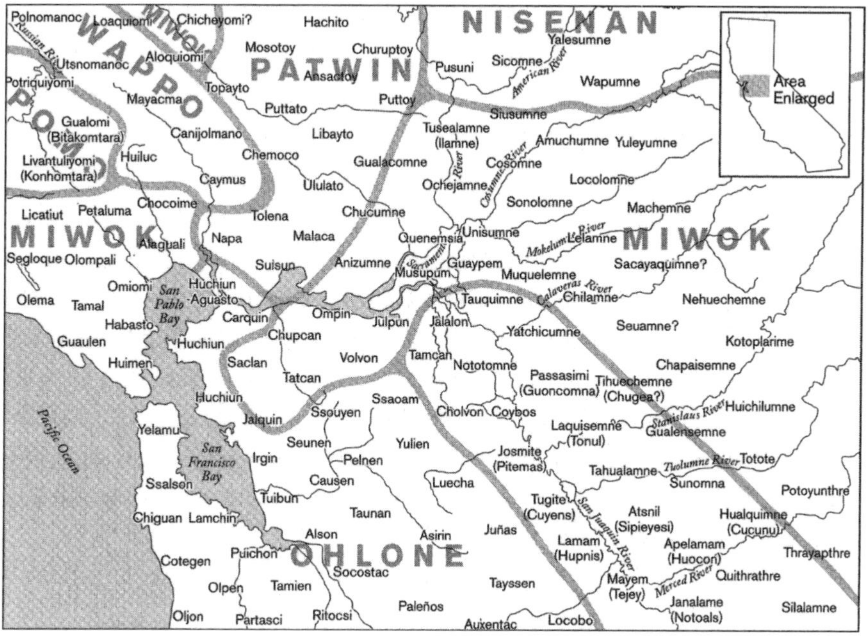

A map indicating the language groups and tribes who lived in West Central California. The Bay Miwok lived in today's northern Contra Costa County. *Randall Milliken, Native Americans in Mission San José.*

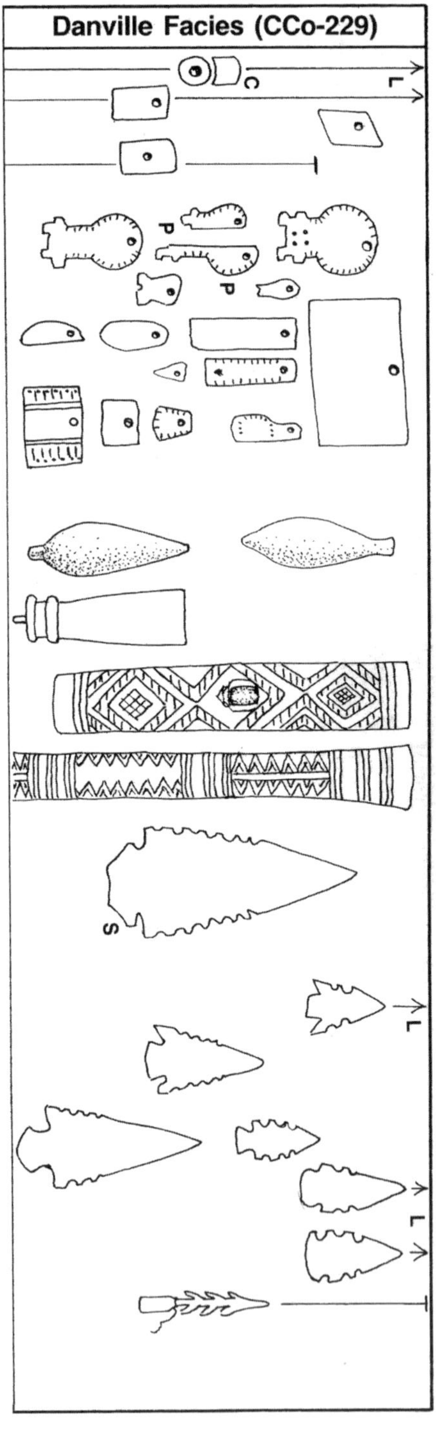

A drawing of artifacts found in a mound on Hartz Avenue. *Smithsonian Institution, Handbook of North American Indians, vol. 8, California.*

Archaeological investigations in Danville have revealed artifacts that speak to the lives of these first people. Some of these investigations took place along Diablo Road (CCo-352), Hartz Avenue (CCo-229), La Gonda Way (CC-539), near Westridge Road (CCo-365), and at the high school in 2009. Dr. David Fredrickson supervised the large CCo-352 investigation between Diablo Road and San Ramon Creek during the 1950s.

Ina Boone Root, a Danville resident for eighty-five years, remembers her father coming across Indian skeletons on their property along the creek in the 1880s. Viola Root and George Wood recalled a University of California, Berkeley excavation of mounds along the creek in the 1930s, which probably included site CCo-229.

Local historian Inez Butz wrote:

> *That Indians dwelled in Danville there is no doubt as a burial mound and remains of sweathouses and utensils have been uncovered in the area between San Ramon Creek and the Union and Seaside service stations (on Hartz Avenue).*
>
> *When I came to Danville in 1946 that community had three small mounds on the west side of the San Ramon Creek along what was originally the county road. I was told they were shell mounds....During the mid-50's the three mounds were bull-dozed down and the loosened dirt was carted away, loaded into trucks, and used as fill all over town. While the bull-dozers were working and in the evenings after work a number of people, myself included, walked the area to rescue any objects of Indian nature exposed on the surface.*

Unearthed physical evidence from long habitation and oral histories provide knowledge about the culture of Native people. Today, descendants work to revive their languages and traditions as they live twenty-first-century lives.

3

THE SPANISH INVASION

After spending hundreds of years exploring and settling in Central America, Spanish soldiers and missionaries invaded Alta California in 1769. Spain's monarch was concerned about the activities of Russian and English explorers in their northwestern frontier and decided to send troops, missionaries, and eventually settlers to the area. Expeditions moved into Indian territory, confronting about eighty separate tribes from San Diego to San Francisco and upending the Native peoples' stable cultures.

An estimated 340,000 Native people speaking 100 different languages lived in Alta California at this time. At first, the Indians were curious about the newcomers. Tribes expected the Spanish would ask for permission to cross their homelands. They were interested in these Spanish explorers' trade goods and new animals and were impressed by their powerful weapons, rituals, and unusual music.

The 1769 Portolá-Serra expedition first entered the homelands of the Kumeyaay people in the San Diego area. The expedition had several purposes: establish a Spanish presence in the area with presidios along the coast, convert Native people to Christianity and make them productive Spanish citizens. The first troops and Franciscan missionaries traveled north to settle at Monterey and then, to their astonishment and delight, discovered the San Francisco Bay.

The Mission Era

It was expected that the Natives would eventually enter the new missions and become the labor source for any settlements. During the Hispanic era, three military presidios and three civilian villages were established by the Spanish soldiers, and twenty-one missions were established by the Franciscans. Written histories of the area's people and environment appeared in diaries as the Spanish invasion spread along the coast.

The first Spanish expeditions to step foot on San Francisco's East Bay included those of Pedro Fages and Father Juan Crespi in 1772 and Juan Bautista de Anza and Father Pedro Font in 1776.

Danville was first described in a diary entry from Father Crespi in 1772:

> *March 31—At six in the morning we set out.... We came to three villages with some little grass houses. As soon as the heathen caught sight of us they ran away, shouting and panic-stricken.... This valley seemed to me to be a charming site for a settlement with all the advantages that are required.*
>
> *April 1—We set out at six, following the same valley in a southerly direction, the excellence of the road continuing, with many trees. This day we covered ten leagues, all by the same valley, all level land, covered with grass and trees, with many and good creeks, and with numerous villages of very gentle and peaceful heathen. It is a very suitable place for a good mission, having good lands, much water, firewood and many heathen.*

The missionaries drew Bay Miwok and other tribes into their orbit. At first, Indians provided food for the mission population from traditional sources and deer hunting; unbaptized people could stay in their villages and work at the missions.

But the mission setting was a disaster for the Natives. Removed from their homelands, where they knew themselves to be integral parts of nature, they were expected to live an entirely different life. For all of them, the work schedules set up by the priests were demoralizing, and punishments were a reality. Single women and girls were housed in dormitories, which became incubators for disease. The Natives had no immunities to foreign diseases such as measles, cholera, and smallpox.

Native people joined the missions after long debates but resisted Western ways and religion on many levels when they did join. Natives in the East Bay, led by the Bay Miwok-speaking Saclans, fought the Spanish in 1795 after

Natives gambling at Mission Dolores, San Francisco, in 1816. *Artist, Louis Choris; Bancroft Library.*

A drawing of vaqueros with Mission San José in the background during the 1826 Beechey expedition to the Bay Area. The drawing is titled *Californian Mode of Catching Cattle with a Distant View of the Mission of St. Joseph. Artist, R.N. Smyth; Bancroft Library.*

suffering illnesses and punishments at a crowded Mission Dolores. Saclans and others killed baptized Natives who were sent to urge their return and threatened people who might help build Mission San José. This resistance lasted for years.

California historian Hubert Howe Bancroft wrote:

> *The Indians...caused more trouble in the region of San Francisco than in any other part of California, the troublesome gentiles (unbaptized Indians) being chiefly those inhabiting what is now known as Alameda and Contra Costa Counties.*

Because of this hostility, Mission San José was founded close to Santa Clara Mission in 1797 instead of in the eastern valleys of Livermore or San Ramon. When most Tatcans finally did join a mission in 1803 and 1804, they went to Mission Dolores, where a measles epidemic killed their children. An estimated 85 percent of the Indians who came into contact with the Spanish died. In one letter, Father Narciso Durán of Mission San José described the Natives "as fragile as glass."

Mission San José was the most successful Bay Area mission, reporting in 1831 that there were two thousand recruits, twelve thousand cattle, thirteen thousand sheep and thirteen thousand horses. It had extensive orchards and vineyards and a large Native orchestra. Danville and the inland valleys were part of Mission San José's grazing and Native outreach area, with cattle and sheep grazing as far north as Concord in dry years.

In an 1855 land case, José María Amador said the San Ramon Creek and Valley were named for a Native sheepherder named Ramon. This was Ramon Nonato (baptized in 1804), who became a Native alcalde at Mission San José. According to mission records, Ramon was an Ohlone-speaking Native named *Usacse* who came from the Souyen tribe in San Ramon.

The Rancho Era

When Mexico won independence from Spain in 1821, changes in the government's policy on land ownership transformed Alta California. The governance of this northern territory was turbulent in the following decades. Spanish-born Father Duran refused to sign a pledge to the new Mexican constitution of 1822.

The missionaries, who had exercised spiritual and physical control over the baptized Natives, were relieved of their temporal responsibilities, and the Indians scattered. Not without controversy, the twenty-one missions were secularized, with Mission San José joining the ranks in 1836.

The rancho era began, with the Mexican government setting up a process which granted former mission lands primarily to retired soldiers. Applicants were required to describe the land, measure boundaries, clarify no other property claims had been made, and build a home on the new rancho. As with the labor at the missions, the rancho work was done by Native vaqueros and workers; without these mission-trained workers, the ranchos could not have survived.

Brands were registered in order to clarify cattle ownership. Previously, nearly all cattle belonged to the mission, and no brands were needed.

With secularization, the Natives dispersed, some to work on the new ranchos or at the pueblo of San José, some to traditional villages in the Central Valley, and some to the multitribal community of Alisal near Pleasanton. Others formed hostile groups in the foothills of Mount Diablo and stole horses and took cattle or sheep for food from the ranchos. Ranchero Juan Briones was killed by some of these Natives when he tried to retrieve stolen livestock in 1840.

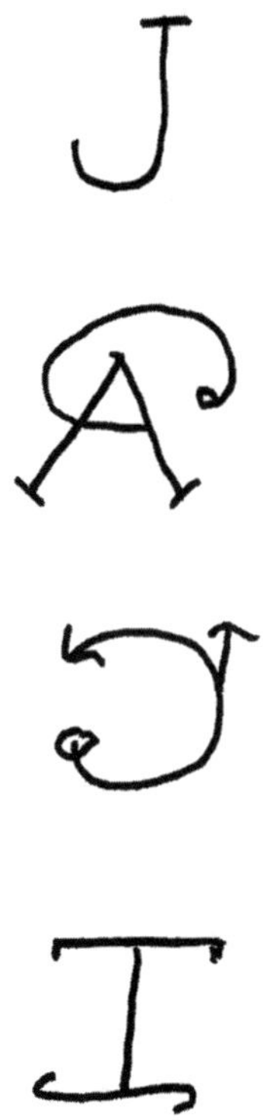

Cattle brands used by (*top to bottom*) Mission San José, Mariano Castro, Bartolome Pacheco, and José María Amador. *Museum of the San Ramon Valley.*

In the 1830s, two Ranchos San Ramon were granted to former soldiers in today's San Ramon Valley, with a third (a *sobrante*, or "leftover") added later. The Rancho San Ramon (Valley) went to Bartolome Pacheco and his nephew Mariano Castro in 1833. It surrounded the San Ramon Creek watershed and covered today's northwestern San Ramon and all of Danville and Alamo.

In 1834, a Rancho San Ramon was granted to José María Amador, this one in today's San Ramon, south of Danville. When Rancho San Ramon is mentioned, writers usually refer to Amador's well-known twenty-thousand-plus-acre spread. His headquarters in today's Dublin had 150 workers who produced leather and wooden products. At one point, his rancho livestock numbered 13,000, along with 300 horses. Perhaps because he was literate,

A couple shown dancing at a fandango. Californios were known for their week-long parties.
Artist, Jo Mora; from Californios: The Saga of the Hard-Riding Vaqueros, America's First Cowboys.

he successfully sold his land to early San Ramon and Dublin pioneers, with the final ten thousand acres going to James Dougherty and a partner. A long oral history at the Bancroft Library, titled *Recollections*, tells his story.

In 1843, brothers Inocencio and José Romero established a rancho in northern Alamo (south to the creek by today's El Serena) and Tice Valley, called Rancho El Sobrante de San Ramon. With the permission of adjacent rancheros, it covered much of Castro's northern section and today's Tice Valley area that surrounds Las Trampas Creek.

Rancho Romero was granted to the brothers subject to a land survey that was planned for 1843. They met most of the requirements—they built an adobe and corrals in Tice Valley and grazed livestock—but they made no survey. When Francisco and José Miguel García wanted to purchase the Alamo section, the Romeros agreed to it, subject to a final confirmation of their title. Francisco built an adobe next to San Ramon Creek, and José Miguel built one farther east.

The Romeros (and therefore, the Garcías) lost ownership of their land in American courts, with the U.S. Supreme Court making the final decision in 1864. Their loss was typical of hundreds of the "unproved" Mexican ranchos throughout the state. Even though the 1848 Mexican-American War treaty guaranteed Mexican land ownership, an American court process which questioned the validity of even long-established ranchos meant few rancheros successfully kept all their land.

In Danville, the Castro-Pacheco Rancho was located west of Mount Diablo in the San Ramon Creek watershed and amounted to two square leagues, or about eight thousand acres. The rancho was divided, with Castro taking the northern half and Pacheco the southern. Around Mount Diablo, the Natives were rustling cattle and were, to say the least, unfriendly. So, the men did not build homes and received permission to live in Santa Clara and Pueblo San José. Roundups brought cattle to their southern boundary (around today's Crow Canyon Road), where rodeos for branding took place. A small redwood house was built near Amador's border for the vaqueros' use.

When Bartolome Pacheco died, his nephew Lorenzo inherited the Pacheco half of the rancho. And after Lorenzo lost his life in an Indian battle, his wife, Rafaela Pacheco y Soto, and their sons inherited this rancho. She ultimately lost the rancho to the notorious American land speculator Horace Carpentier.

In 1846, the Mexican-American War seemed far away, even though there were skirmishes and some battles in Alta California. The Treaty of

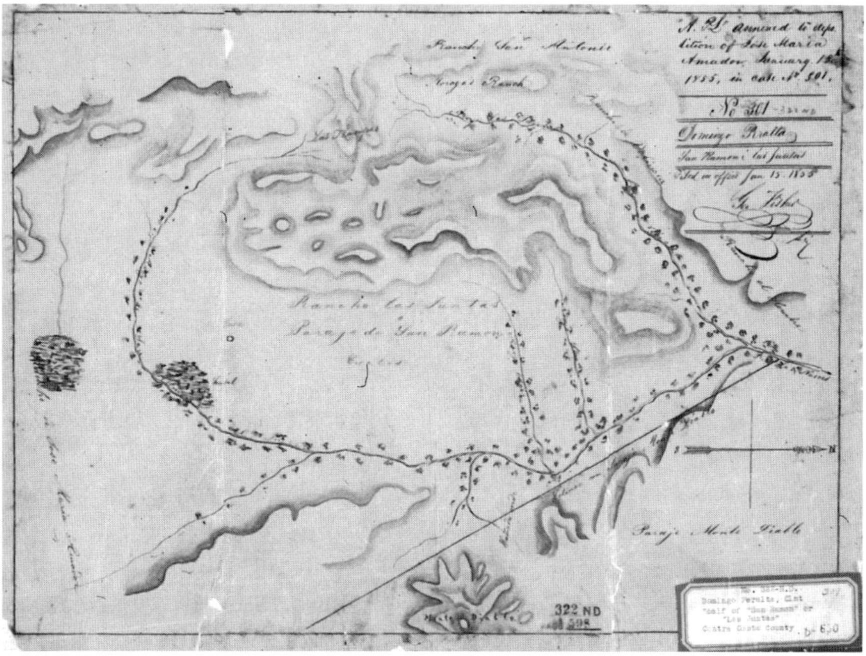

This hand-drawn map (*diseno*) shows the Castro/Pacheco Rancho San Ramon, with north situated to the right. It shows San Ramon Creek and its tributaries, Las Trampas Hills and Mount Diablo. *Bancroft Library.*

Guadalupe-Hidalgo ceded much of the West, including California, to the United States on February 2, 1848. An estimated fourteen thousand non-Native people lived in California at the time. Two weeks earlier, gold had been discovered at Sutter's Mill in Coloma, setting off a massive Gold Rush that transformed Alta California.

The California Gold Rush brought hundreds of thousands of miners and settlers to the new state, including the founders of Danville.

4

GOLD IN THE HILLS AND VALLEY

1850–1870

A treaty with Mexico transferred Alta California to the United States in early 1848, soon after gold was discovered in the Sierra Nevada. Thousands of miners arrived from all over the world and transformed rural California. Skipping the usual territorial phase, California won statehood on September 9, 1850. The state's population boomed to over three hundred thousand in the 1850s.

Fresh from the grueling work of gold mining, early pioneers found another treasure in Danville's sparsely populated broad meadows and tree-lined creeks. It was an ideal place to settle. Rancher Robert O. Baldwin wrote, "The land in the valley is unsurpassed by any in the state."

Although the treaty with Mexico guaranteed Mexican property rights, the vast rancho grasslands looked vacant and available to the immigrants. Familiar with the practice of western homesteading, these settlers claimed squatters' rights, marked property boundaries, built homes, and planted crops. Some did try to find the rancho owners. This lack of clear ownership produced major title problems later.

Settling In

Immigrants came to the Danville area early. Scots John and Elizabeth Smith and their son Jimmy started a farm in 1850 just south of the future

The Mendenhall/Wood house, built by pioneer William "Philp" Mendenhall in 1853, still stands at the Wood Ranch headquarters in Sycamore Valley. *Museum of the San Ramon Valley.*

village. In Sycamore Valley, Leonard Eddy built a small place in 1850, and William "Philip" Mendenhall had constructed a two-story house there by 1853. Andrew and Daniel Inman settled Green Valley in 1852. Charles and Cynthia Wood purchased Mendenhall's property in 1862.

R.O. Baldwin and William Meese arrived in 1852 and bought what they called "squatters rights" to begin farming south of Danville in 1853. Elmer and Livia Cox and their family began a ranch near the Meese spread in 1853.

Elmer Cox was the county education superintendent for the area from 1856 to 1859. He and his wife were also active in the 1870s women's suffrage efforts and joined the county's California Woman Suffrage Association. Perhaps they supported this cause because they had five daughters. Three of them, Mary, Sarah, and Panthea, married Danville ranchers R.O. Baldwin, John Larabee, and William Meese, respectively.

When Dan Inman purchased the property that became Danville's village in 1858, it was located in a pivotal spot at the intersection of the county road (later Front Street) with Camino Tassajara (now Diablo Road). There was probably a bridge at this location early on.

The Danville Hotel and Post Office, run by Henry W. Harris, was located at the northwest corner of the two roads. As the first postmaster (from 1860 to 1865), Harris reported that, on January 1, 1862, there were twenty people

Top: Pioneers Robert O. and Mary Cox Baldwin, who came to Danville in the 1850s, managed the Osage Ranch and had six children. *Museum of the San Ramon Valley.*

Bottom: Danville Grammar School on Front Street, with teacher A.J. Young on the right. He taught Danville students from 1880 to 1900. *Museum of the San Ramon Valley.*

residing in the town proper, with two hundred people in the vicinity voting in the last election. By then, there was a general store, blacksmith, wheelwright, and hotel in town.

In 1866, Michael and Matilda Cohen built a house in the popular Gothic Revival style on Front Street, near their general store. The builder was Nathaniel Howard. They were French immigrants whose three children were born in America. Michael had become a citizen in Ohio in 1851, belonged to Masonic Lodge No. 122 in Alamo and was postmaster from 1865 to 1886. In 1864, the Cohens' store advertised cutlery, groceries, glass ware, tobacco, paints, rope, and a variety of farmers' and mechanics' tools.

The first high school in the county, the Union Academy, was located between Danville and Alamo from 1860 to 1868. Early grammar school classes were held in homes, with the large Howard home in Green Valley providing a room for the area's first school. Three early grammar schools were built in the Danville area: Danville (1858), Green Valley (1865), and Sycamore (1866).

Camp Meetings

In the 1850s, people began talking about founding churches, and some religious camp meetings were organized, according to Mary Ann Jones in her autobiography. She wrote, "Soon we began to think about building a church. Well, we must have a camp meeting....The time and place was decided upon." She bragged, "[A]nd we held a meeting and we had a good one!"

The location of the camp meeting was a field west of San Ramon Creek at the border of Alamo and Danville. On a hill east of the creek, a cemetery was established, with little Callie Chrisman's interment marking the first recorded burial in 1856.

A boy at the time, James Smith recalled that several meetings were held each fall beginning in the mid-1850s. Hundreds of people came. Four or five preachers took turns speaking each morning, afternoon and evening for seven full days. Smith recorded, "[P]eople came prepared to camp and stay a week" from Napa, Alameda, Santa Clara, and Sonoma Sounties, as well as the "distant parts of Contra Costa."

Smith also wrote that converts were brought to be baptized in the creek, washed of their sins:

I saw many young women baptized in my old swimming hole but never saw a man or boy baptized—to be washed clean of their sins, they were usually sent to jail to repent.

The local church members employed Mack, a negro cook, who lived near Alamo to prepare barbecued meats for all, also coffee. The local people would bring bread, cakes and pies, and a table was prepared for any not otherwise prepared for, so none might go hungry.

I heard some wonderful exhorters at different times—they painted the fiery pit with the living coals ready to consume the sinner, in fervid and glowing terms. In later years I attended a negro camp meeting in Oakland and heard some wonderful preaching and singing…But the religious fervor did not compare with those I had attended by San Ramon Creek.

Western writer Bret Harte lived to the east, in the Tassajara Valley, serving as a tutor for four ranch boys in 1856. It is likely that his book *First Family of Tassajara* and fanciful tale "The Legend of Mount Diablo" reflect his stay. In another story, "An Apostle of the Tules," Harte describes a camp meeting as having a "singular resemblance to a circus," with "smaller tents which served for prayer meetings, classrooms known to the few unbelievers as 'sideshows.'"

THE 1860S: A CHALLENGING TIME

This decade was an eventful one, with floods, land title battles, a major earthquake, and Civil War discord.

San Ramon Creek flooded during the mega-storm of 1861–62. That winter, the *Contra Costa Gazette* reported, "The San Ramon Valley was one sheet of water from hill to hill as far as the eye could see." In the town's early years, water supplies came from springs, wells, and San Ramon Creek and its tributaries. San Ramon Creek influenced village development when it occasionally washed out the creek bank and undermined buildings along Front Street.

Opposite: This map records the final ownerships of property in 1865, purchased from the notorious land speculator Horace Carpentier, who was called a "land fiend" by H.H. Bancroft. *Museum of the San Ramon Valley.*

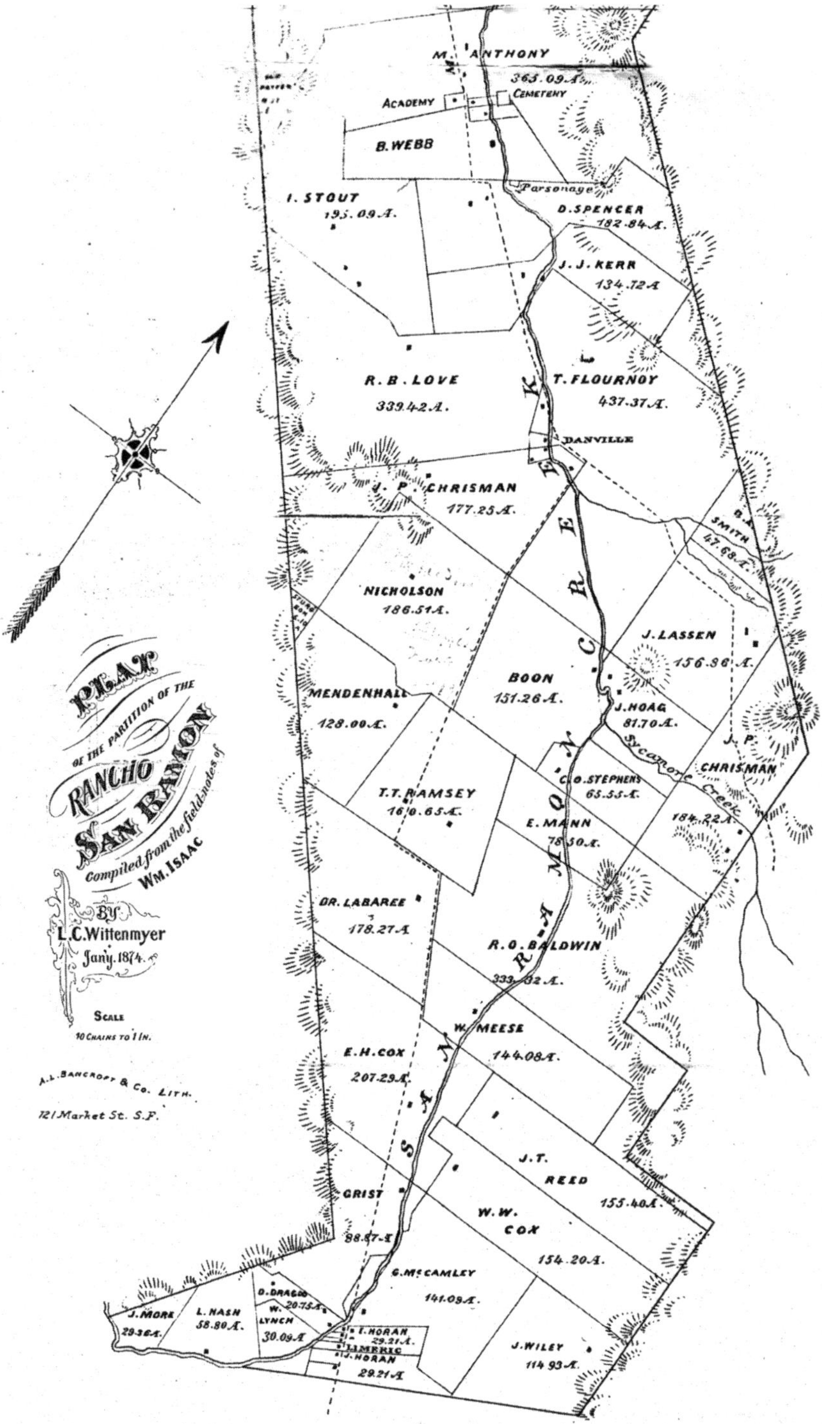
M. ANTHONY
363.09 A.
ACADEMY
CEMETERY
B. WEBB
Parsonage
I. STOUT
195.09 A.
D. SPENCER
182.84 A.
J. J. KERR
134.72 A
R. B. LOVE
339.42 A.
T. FLOURNOY
437.37 A.
DANVILLE
J. P. CHRISMAN
177.25 A.
SAN RAMON CREEK
G. A. SMITH
47.68 A.
NICHOLSON
186.51 A.
J. LASSEN
156.36 A.
BOON
151.26 A.
MENDENHALL
128.00 A.
J. HOAG
81.70 A.
Sycamore Creek
J. P. CHRISMAN
184.22 A.
C. O. STEPHENS
65.55 A.
T. T. RAMSEY
160.65 A.
E. MANN
78.50 A.
DR. LABAREE
178.27 A.
R. O. BALDWIN
333.32 A.
W. MEESE
144.08 A.
E. H. COX
207.29 A.
J. T. REED
155.40 A.
GRIST
88.87 A.
W. W. COX
154.20 A.
G. McCAMLEY
141.09 A.
J. MORE
29.36 A.
L. NASH
58.80 A.
D. DRAGGO
20.75 A.
W. LYNCH
30.09 A.
E. HORAN
29.21 A.
LIMERIC
J. HORAN
29.21 A.
J. WILEY
114.93 A.
PLAT OF THE PARTITION OF THE RANCHO SAN RAMON
Compiled from the field-notes of WM. ISAAC
BY L. C. Wittenmyer
Jany. 1874.
Scale
10 Chains to 1 In.
A. L. Bancroft & Co. Lith.
721 Market St. S.F.

LAND TITLES

Land ownership was insecure for years after people settled in. Through various means, Horace Carpentier had acquired the entire Alamo/Danville San Ramon Rancho from its Mexican owners. Conversations with the unscrupulous attorney found he increased the costs to ranchers each time they tried to negotiate. Historian Hubert Bancroft described Carpentier as a "shrewd land fiend."

Litigation finally came to an end in 1865 and provided clear titles for the settlers. Sixty-five ranchers agreed to pay Carpentier $90,000 in gold coin over a period of four years, with interest set at 1 percent per month.

The San Ramon Grant case was written up in newspapers and the Congressional Record. A plat map from County Recorder L.C. Wittenmyer showed the ranchers' names and properties, which, in Danville, included Baldwin, Meese, Cox, Chrisman, Larabee, Love, Flournoy, and Mendenhall. Many spoke bitterly about having to pay for their land twice.

THE EARTHQUAKE OF 1868

The *Contra Costa Gazette*, on October 24, 1868, reported on the huge Hayward quake that had occurred three days earlier: "The one-story brick store belonging to Mr. Peel, at Danville lost a part of its front wall." The Alamo Masonic Lodge's brick building and both original Garcia adobes were destroyed. The writer opined, "People generally are inclined to adopt the comfortable conclusion that nature will require a long period of repose after so great a labor and will not soon disturb us again with such a spasm."

Charlotte Wood wrote that 1868 was a memorable year "because of the big earthquake." Her mother, Cynthia, said this quake moved from east to west and skimmed the milk in the Wood Ranch milk house. She recorded:

> *Father and sister Libbie were in San Francisco that morning, and when they returned home that evening (hurrying out of the city as best they could with the confusion and excitement of the catastrophe), they found some of the neighbors there, beds made up on the dining room floor. But no one slept.*

The Civil War in Danville: 1860–1865

Civil War disagreements disrupted July Fourth celebrations, conversations and political campaigns. Most settlers were immigrants from the East Coast and brought with them their political opinions. Many in the San Ramon Valley were from the southern states of Kentucky and Tennessee and the slave state of Missouri, while others hailed from Massachusetts, Illinois, and points north. The county and the state were pro-Union, and people took sides with few nuanced opinions.

The Inman brothers firmly thought that states had the right to secede. In Green Valley, Andrew Inman's mother-in-law had a Black servant who was surely once enslaved. Andrew represented the county in the state assembly in 1856 and in the state senate from 1860 to 1862. But when the county's Democratic Convention nominated Daniel Inman for sheriff in 1863, he lost by a vote of 1,006 to 528.

After Charles and Cynthia Wood moved to Sycamore Valley in 1862, their daughter Charlotte wrote, "It being early Civil War times, there were many sympathizers with both the North and the South, and naturally there was a little hesitancy in meeting new comers, so no one called on Mother during her first six months here." The Woods were "strong Northerners" who hailed from Massachusetts.

Lincoln and Johnson Club members from the valley in 1864 included David Glass, Charles Howard, James Foster, J.R. McDonald, and A.W. Hammett. Other active local Union Republicans were the Crows, Levi and Sarah Maxcy, Edwin Cox, Henry Hawxhurst, and R.G. Davis.

James Smith recalled several events which reflected the conflict. One was a political rally at the fairgrounds in Pacheco early in the 1860s. He pointed out the involvement of active pro-secession Democrats John Snydor, Jesse Bowles, and the Inman brothers. Bowles organized a parade from Danville, which featured a large log with the name "Constitution" painted on each side. Loaded on a wagon, the log had a huge maul (hammer) with the name "Lincoln" printed on it. Smith wrote, "This was to indicate that Lincoln was driving his advisors to split the Constitution of the United States."

The Fourth of July 1864 provided some more memorable moments related to the Civil War, which Smith also described. Finis E. Johnson was chosen to commit the Declaration to memory and recite it as part of the program. That day, he had not proceeded far before one of the (very pro-Union) Crow family members rose and, in forceful language, asserted, "No

A portrait of President Abraham Lincoln. Civil War debates over Lincon's determination to save the Union roiled Danville. *Public domain.*

secession speech shall be delivered here" and followed with more strong language. With that, the event ended, and people dispersed.

The *Contra Costa Gazette* wrote up this rowdy July Fourth ending: "[L]et the cry go forth that there is yet in San Ramon valley enough patriots to protect themselves from insult, and protect the institutions for our Government from being vilified by travelling one horse secesh politicians."

Republicans in the valley supported Abraham Lincoln and the Union and raised funds for the Sanitary Commission. Edwin Cox, who hailed from Indiana, chaired the county's Union Republican Convention in 1864. That autumn, a huge Union rally was held in Danville in Flournoy's field (around today's Danville Oak), which was covered extensively by a *Gazette* writer on October 8, 1964 in an article titled "The Union Gathering":

> *The largest and most respectably attended meeting ever witnessed in San Ramon Valley, was held on Saturday, October 1st, under the shady oaks in the field adjoining the residence of Thomas Flournoy, Esq., by the union party of Contra Costa county.*
>
> *Hon. J.F. Swift, first addressed the meeting, who gave the assemblage to understand that nothing but the re-election of Lincoln and Johnson would satisfy the majority of all thinking men. He was followed by hon. Frank Pixley, who gave one of his good sound sense speeches, which made some of the Democratic worshippers pull long faces, and the meeting broke up with three cheers for Lincoln and Johnson. The Union League made an excellent appearance with their fife and drum, and starry banners, and were loudly cheered. DANVILLE.*

Since Danville was a hotbed of prominent Democratic support, the Republicans may have set up this rally to get in their opponents' faces. In Danville, the presidential vote in November 1864 supported George McClellan, with 91 votes for McClellan and 76 for Lincoln. It was one of only two communities in the county that voted against the president's re-election.

Life in Danville wasn't all Civil War arguments, as people supported their one-room schools and the Union Academy and attended May Day celebrations, potlucks, dances, and graduation events. And there were always picnics and trips to Mount Diablo's summit.

By the end of the 1860s, the population in the Danville and Lafayette areas was nearly 1,800. The prominent Danville Hotel, opened in 1858, burned down in 1873. The small village was surrounded by acres of hay and grains, grazing land, and almond orchards. California in this period was known as the "granary of the world," and commercial crops of wheat were planted throughout the valley. Road conditions meant grain transport to Martinez or Port Costa was a labor-intensive day-long trek.

Recovering from title and Civil War disputes, R.O. Baldwin clearly loved the valley, writing in the *Gazette*, "I came to this valley thirty-five years ago. I thought it then was the Eden of the State and I have no reason to change my mind since."

5

CREATING A COMMUNITY

Betterment of the community was on people's mind, as the Civil War schisms and title uncertainties were left behind. Founders organized schools and churches, served on school boards, planned picnics, and shared new farm techniques. Some of the settler names appeared regularly as these leaders, among them Charles Wood, Robert O. Baldwin, William Meese, Robert Love, and Albert J. Young.

Nineteenth-century businesses and new civic buildings were clustered along Front Street, the town's main street until about 1910. People needed these educational, civic, and religious buildings and activities to create a community.

Praise for Danville's setting often appeared in newspapers. In 1887, the *Pacific Rural Press* quoted Grange lecturer Charles Wood as saying that people in Danville "have reveled for years in its genial, health-giving climate, and enjoyed the unfailing products of its soil....No more secluded and pretty place...could [be] found within a day's ride of San Francisco."

Schools

The Union Academy was a boarding and day school on Danville's border with Alamo. The Cumberland Presbyterian Church had worked to find a location for such a high school, but when a committee chose Pacheco, no

This is a drawing of the Union Academy, a high school located at the boundary of Danville and Alamo. It was described by academy student James Smith in 1926. *Museum of the San Ramon Valley.*

school appeared. Alamo and Danville leaders created the Contra Costa Education Association, built a large school, and hired Reverend David McClure as its director. Local students could travel to the school and did not have to board.

It was the first high school in the entire county and was housed in a large, three-story building. Opening in 1860, the academy's advanced curriculum taught Latin, Greek, mathematics, and literature, as well as calisthenics, vocal music, French, and Spanish. Music (with use of instruments), drawing, and painting were taught for an extra charge. The charge for a high school student who boarded there was thirty-two dollars a month.

Some parents were critical of the "extras." But Reverend McClure stated that he was directed to run the school "upon the most approved methods of conducting Academies in the United States…and never expected to be regulated by the opinions of people in which the Union Academy is located." Trustees Robert Love, John Jones, and Silas Stone supported McClure.

Young Jimmy Smith attended the academy, since his parents sent him to every school available. Later, he wrote in detail about the school building and his experiences there, including this account of a monthly party:

> *They played games, danced to the Virginia Reel, Money Musk and cotillions with Rev. McClure playing the violin and instructing us in the intricacies of the different steps. At the conclusion of the dance we were furnished a light repast. We were then asked to kneel and our teacher would offer a prayer, after which we were dismissed….Did we love our teacher? I'll testify we did.*

The academy lasted until 1868, when it burned down in the summer, leaving the valley with no local high school for four decades.

Danville's first grammar school had rocky beginnings. A country schoolhouse was built in 1858 south of town. Then a new one was constructed in the village in 1867 but burned down soon after. In 1870, the original school was moved to Front Street, south of the Grange Hall. It was replaced in 1896. R.O. Baldwin served on the Danville Grammar School Board his entire life.

Robert Burgess, the son of Danville's Presbyterian church pastor, wrote in his *Memoirs*:

> *In 1893 I was graduated from grammar school. The school was a one-room affair with an anteroom in which the girls hung up their hats, etc. The boys hung up their hats on nails along the schoolroom walls—in those days we wore hats. The teacher was Mr. A.J. Young. He was a fine man, and also taught our Sunday School. He was the entire staff and carried us through eight grades, ending with algebra.*

Above: A new, impressive Danville Grammar School was built in 1896 on Front Street. *Museum of the San Ramon Valley.*

Following spread: A Grange chromolithograph. This poster, which shows a Grange meeting, was sold to Granges countrywide in the nineteenth century. *Museum of the San Ramon Valley.*

A.J. Young taught at the two Danville schools from 1883 to 1900 and, as head of Christian education at the Presbyterian church, was an influential and rather severe presence in young peoples' lives.

Danville Grammar School District voters supported a $5,000 bond to build a new school in 1895. An 1895 *Contra Costa Gazette* article described peoples' hopes for the school:

> *We want our school house to be one of the most prominent buildings in the valley, located on such a street and facing in a direction to attract attention from any transient traveler or tourist through our valley. Let everyone know we have an interest in education by looking at the building.*

In 1896, this impressive new grammar school was dedicated with a grand ceremony.

Two other one-room schools were established in in the Danville vicinity in Green Valley (1865) on Andrew Inman's land and in Sycamore Valley (1866) on land from Wade Hayes. Charlotte Wood walked from their ranch to attend the Sycamore School and taught there for thirty-one years, from 1890 to 1921.

The entire San Ramon Valley had six grammar school districts in the nineteenth century, supported by taxpayers in each school district. They were Alamo, Danville, Green Valley, San Ramon, Sycamore and Tassajara.

The Danville Grange No. 85: Patrons of Husbandry

In the 1870s ranchers were talking about ways to improve crop production and the challenges of high bank charges and railroad rates. A farmers' union was started, which, on a motion by Robert Baldwin, included both women and men. On May 5, 1873, San Ramon's George McCamley and Danville's Baldwin went to San Francisco for a convention with plans to create a statewide farmers' union. An invigorating speaker, W.H. Baxter convinced convention members that joining the National Grange, Patrons of Husbandry, would serve their needs. Attendees were intrigued, then convinced, and decided to establish Granges throughout California.

A Danville Grange was founded in 1873, the eighty-fifth in the state. There were thirty charter members, ten women and twenty men, which included

GRANGE OF PA
LIBERTY.
Entered according to act of Congress A.D.1874 by the AMERICAN OLEOGRAPH CO. in the Office of the Librarian of the House of Congress,

OF HUSBANDRY.
JUSTICE.
Washington D.C.
Published by the AMERICAN OLEOGRAPH CO. Milwaukee Wis.
Kurz.

three couples, Cynthia and Charles Wood, Mary and Robert Baldwin, and James and Sally Boone. Charles Wood became the first worthy master, as enthusiasm for the new group spread throughout the valley and state.

At first, they met in the Danville Grammar School, which they soon outgrew. Next, they raised funds for a new Grange Hall to be placed west of Front Street. Brother C.E. Howard was put in charge of the construction. Grangers first met at the new hall on November 14, 1874.

The Grange became the heart of activity in the valley; initially, it held Saturday meetings and gathered families to share dinner baskets. And there were always large Christmas and harvest celebrations. Grange historian Inez Butz wrote:

> *Into this dull life of the farmer and his family the Grange brought social contacts, news of the outside world, and the pleasure of laughing, talking and eating with new and old friends and neighbors. Programs were an established item in the order of business and people who had never spoken, sung, or debated before an audience could now have that opportunity.*

Charles and Cynthia Rice Wood moved to Sycamore Valley in 1862. They became Grange leaders in 1873, when both were charter members. *Wood family archives.*

During the nineteenth century, the Grange was the glue that held the community together. "Being the only public meeting place in all the valley, the Grange Hall became the center of all social, political and public activities. The spirit of this early Grange was outstanding in its zeal for the betterment of every phase of the community life," wrote Worthy Master Will Stewart.

Addressing issues of importance to farmers, state Grangers hired their own wheat agent, created a bank and business association, and set up a facility for storing and shipping grain. They worked to reduce railroad charges, address squirrel infestations, and share knowledge about new agricultural practices. Locally, their programs addressed the need for a railroad, a new high school, a library and better roads.

In the 1870s, the Grange bought cotton sacks for grain in large volumes and eliminated some of the middleman costs. Buyers insisted on sacked wheat for shipment on the sailing ships.

In 1912, one of the original charter members, Cynthia Wood, wrote:

> *The members of 39 years ago who have fewer neighbors and fewer opportunities for gathering in a social way can better understand the good the Grange has done in bringing together the total strangers of that time and uniting them like a family in bonds of friendship that may not be severed while time lasts. Besides the pleasant social joys of the Grange, its educational benefits are great in leading our agricultural community to consider its own needs and the way to ensure its rights.*

Churches Are Founded

Reverend R.S. Symington wrote a history of the first Danville church building in the 1882 *History of Contra Costa County*. In it, he recounts the events which led to the founding of the Danville Presbyterian Church.

In the 1870s, there were several Protestant groups in the valley, including Christian, Congregational, Methodist-Episcopal and Cumberland Presbyterian. The San Francisco Presbytery began sending ministers to the county in the 1850s. Reverend McClure held Sunday Presbyterian services beginning in 1857 and then focused his attention on the academy. No church was organized, although Sunday church services were held at the Union Academy. People met for services at homes and the Danville Grammar School.

The handsome New England–style Presbyterian church served the community from 1876 to 1932. *Museum of the San Ramon Valley.*

In 1875, Protestants held meetings and resolved to erect a house of worship in Danville. Since a pastor would be needed to lead any church, those present agreed to elect a pastor and pledge funds to pay him—and they agreed to accept whoever was elected, no matter what denomination they were. They chose Reverend Symington from the San José Presbytery as the first pastor.

Funds for the church building came from the Presbyterian Board of Home Missions and local subscriptions. It was not an easy effort. Nevertheless, the worshipers proceeded to build the church at a cost of $6,500. The church was designed by architect Charles Giddis of San Francisco and built by C.E. Dunchu, with the cornerstone laid on October 1, 1875.

When the church was ready to be dedicated, the trustees announced that there was still a debt of $2,500 to be paid prior to any such ceremony. People stretched to do this with subscriptions from $50 to $250, but they were still short $165. Then, according to the 1882 history, "a gentleman who had been watching the whole scene with marked interest…broke the silence and said, 'Clerk, tell them the debt is paid.'" A Baptist who lived some distance from Danville had saved the day. Symington wrote, "It was the happiest day ever known in Danville."

Finally, the lovely New England–style Danville Presbyterian Church was dedicated on June 18, 1876. The first trustees were R.O. Baldwin, J.J. Kerr, and David Glass. One of the initial elders was Albert J. Young, who served as the clerk of the session for fifty years.

Reverend Symington wrote the following about the church:

> *The building of this house of worship is an epoch in the history of the church. It locates the interests of this people. It is a home for the Christian's soul. It is a moral educator. It stands with its spire constantly pointing to Heaven, every day bearing its silent testimony for God. Every traveler marks it. Every journal in the land notices it. Every pious man seeking a home is influenced by it.*

Historians like to point out the first Catholic mass in the area was celebrated in 1772, provided by Father Juan Crespi when the first Spanish expedition camped in Danville. Most Portuguese and Irish immigrants to the area were Catholic. Visiting priests served the faithful for years in their homes, and Mission San José (twenty miles away) served as a parish church.

In 1910, a new Catholic parish was established, which included expansive boundaries, including Livermore, Pleasanton, Concord, Moraga, and Orinda. The handsome St. Isidore Catholic Church was built at the southeast corner

This is the first St. Isidore Catholic Church, built on Hartz Avenue in Danville in 1911. *Museum of the San Ramon Valley.*

of Linda Mesa and Hartz Avenue in Danville and dedicated on July 28, 1912. St. Isidore is the saint of farmers.

Before the building was completed, Father John Collins gave mass in the 1874 Grange Hall and lived at the Danville Hotel.

LIBRARIES

In the 1800s, books were rare and precious. Several families had home libraries, such as the Stones, Baldwins, and Woods. They valued education and probably loaned their books to others.

The first library in the valley was started when the Danville Grange applied to receive a traveling book service from the California State Library in 1906. In that program, fifty books were loaned to individuals for three months. Granger Mary Podva applied for the books, and in 1910, she and Mary More were the librarians.

Civic buildings, such as Danville's Grange Hall (1874), the Presbyterian church (1876), and two grammar schools (1870 and 1896), with adjacent local businesses made Front Street the center of the community for decades.

6

AN AGRARIAN CENTURY

While Spanish diarists described the countryside as a wilderness, Indians had managed the land for eons. They set fires to promote desired seeds and nurture new growth, pruned for basket materials, and dug for edible bulbs, such as soap root. When the Spanish introduced cattle and sheep, which grazed the meadows and brought nonnative seeds on their coats, these traditional Native habitats were destroyed.

Soon after the Gold Rush, former miners discovered that in California, they could make a good living ranching or farming. In no time, they successfully mastered the region's Mediterranean-like weather patterns. In 1861, surveyor William H. Brewer was impressed: "The San Ramon Valley, west of Mount Diablo, lay at our feet, the richest and most lovely I have yet seen in the state."

Often involved beyond Danville, ranchers Jessie Bowles and Edwin Cox helped organize the Contra Costa Agricultural Society in 1859, which created the first county fair. Later, locals took leadership positions in the Grange, Cattlemen's Association, the Farm Bureau, and Cowbelles.

The *Contra Costa Gazette*, on February 17, 1894, waxed poetic in an article titled "Danville, a Town with an Assured Prosperous Future":

> *Nature put the townsite of Danville in a favored spot in this highly favored county of ours. Every variety of farm production of the temperate and semi-tropic zones can be grown there. Much of the land is now held in quite large tracts, but there is a disposition to divide and sell. When this*

is done…here will grow the cereals, the grape, the olive, the fig, the prune, the apricot, almonds especially making a profitable yield, young orchards yielding over a quarter tons to the acre.

Eucalyptus trees were broadly introduced in the 1860s as fast-growing trees that could be used for windbreaks and lumber, though the latter use turned out to be very limited. Charlotte Wood recalled her father planting boxes of "thrifty-looking little blue plants six or eight inches high."

Winter rains were interspersed with periodic droughts. In the early 1860s, huge floods swept the valley, carrying barns and livestock away. Farmers always talked about water—how much or how little there was and how the crops were responding. Ranchers with water rights placed floodgates on the creeks, creating ponds with which to water walnut trees and other crops from April to October. The gates would be open during the rainy season. Only the large Bishop Ranch south of Danville had enough water to irrigate its crops. Everywhere else there were springs and wells were dug with windmills, elevated water tanks, and pumps set up to serve the house, animals and vegetable gardens.

CATTLE COUNTRY

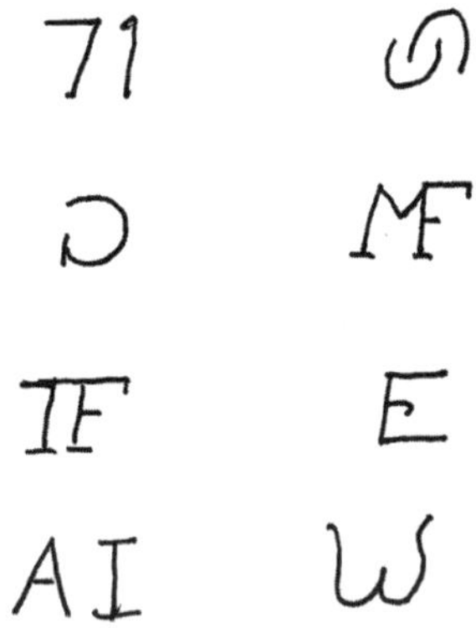

Cattle grazed on the hills well into the twenty-first century. While the Hispanic ranchers did not actively improve their stock, since hides were the important commercial product, post–Gold Rush beef became a cash product. Albert Ward Stone and others brought cattle with them in expeditions across the plains. The new breeds were usually "British" beef breeds—Hereford, Angus, and Shorthorn. Charles J. Wood is given credit for bringing the first Angus cattle to the area in the 1930s and for being a prime mover in organizing the Contra Costa–Alameda Cattlemen's Association in 1945.

Hay was an important product, since each cow or horse needed a ton of hay for summer feed. Eventually, the valley's forage for cattle, with wild

Opposite: Brands from Danville ranchers (*from top to bottom*): R.O. Baldwin, Hap Magee, E.H. Cox, William Meese, Thomas Flournoy, Ed Rasmussen, Andrew Inman, and Charles Wood. *Museum of the San Ramon Valley.*

Above: Angus cattle in a corral on the Wood Ranch, with ranch buildings in the background. *Wood family archives.*

oats on the hills and native clover in the area, was renowned throughout the country.

In 1924, a foot-and-mouth plague devastated cattle herds throughout California. Hundreds of head of cattle had to be shot and buried to get rid of the disease and many herds were reduced by half.

Wheat and Other Grains

James Smith recalled his father, John "Scotch" Smith, raising a little patch of wheat in 1850 and threshing it with a flail. Next, he grew several wheat crops, each with improving technologies. At his ranch, R.O. Baldwin estimated a wheat yield at thirty to forty bushels an acre in 1887, reduced from earlier yields that were as high as eighty bushels. Farmers did not use fertilizers or rotate crops, depleting the soil.

The *California Farmer* proclaimed in 1869, "California is now the esteemed granary of the world," with its hard, dry white wheat popular on the

Horses powered this Wood Ranch wheat thrasher in the 1890s. *Wood family archives.*

Liverpool corn exchange. Baldwin made his first shipment of wheat, 150 tons, by rail to Port Costa on the Carquinez Strait in June 1891. In the 1880s, Contra Costa County produced half of all the grain leaving California.

Harvesting the vast hillsides of grains and hay took an entire community and often contract laborers. The 1880 census listed fifty-seven Chinese laborers who harvested in Green Valley. Other seasonal workers were "Gypsy," Japanese, "Okie," Filipino and Mexican. Cookhouses were used to feed workers two breakfasts, two lunches and dinner. The Woods employed a Japanese cook during the harvest.

THE DIVERSIFIED RANCH

Local ranchers constantly tried out different crops to find which would work commercially. R.O. Baldwin was always experimenting. At the Contra Costa Fair in 1874, Baldwin won a first-place prize for the best Mangel Wurtzel beets. The fair report in the 1874 *Pacific Rural Press* also acknowledged the fine horses produced by Baldwin and the lambs, ewes, and bucks shown by W.Z. Stone.

Judge W.W. Cope of Green Valley was renowned for having "the finest almond orchards in the state," according to the *Gazette* in 1887. He had sixty acres of almond trees, with vineyards and orchards of apricot, pear, and plum trees.

Top: This large cow barn was acquired by Charles J. Wood in 1912. It was dismantled at the Oakwood Park Stock Farm and rebuilt on the Wood Ranch. *Wood Ranch archives.*

Bottom: This drawing from the *Pacific Rural Press* (May 14, 1887) depicts Libbie Wood tending the elaborate Wood Ranch cream separator. *Wood family archives.*

The Woodside Ranch in Sycamore Valley was also well known, eventually growing to 1,200 acres. It was founded by Charles and Cynthia Wood and managed by three more generations of ranchers: Charles J. (1890s–1942), George (1942–68) and Don (1968–2023). The *Pacific Rural Press*, in 1887, described the ranch as a prime example of diversified farming with a dairy, modern improvements in the stock farm, two hundred Leghorn chickens (tended by Charlotte Wood) and 200 acres of grain. Over the decades, they ran cattle and nurtured orchards, which yielded apples, prunes, plums, pears, peaches, apricots, grapes, and almonds.

Many ranchers had a few milk cows and sold butter and/or cream as a year-round source of income. Often, the farm women were in charge of the cows and tended the chickens for eggs, which brought cash to the ranches. Cream was an important income product, and a system of cream production and marketing began in the nineteenth century. The Danville Creamery was located on School Street not long after the train arrived in 1891. The Woods had a large dairy herd and delivered and sold cream in Hayward once a week in the 1880s.

There were several local dairies over the years, including Kamp's on Blackhawk Road and the Morgan and McNeil Dairies. The Mount Diablo Dairy in Danville (owned by James Root and H.H. Daley) advertised, "Pure Milk & Cream Delivered from T.B. Tested Herd."

Vineyards and Fruits

In an 1892 *Gazette* article, B.W. Stone wrote about the advisability of planting vines on the hillside in soil which was "unusually mellow and loose." He averaged over $100 per acre from his vineyards. In Green Valley, the Cope Ranch had orchards and vineyards, and the Henry Brothers had three thousand vines that yielded table grapes described as "among the finest flavored in the state."

The Ralph and Wilfred Harrison Ranch was featured in a 1926 Byron Development publication:

> *Cherry trees more than thirty-two years old produce luxuriantly. Mr. Harrison has established record productions for Royal Annes. Beautifully colored and finely flavored Carmen peaches thrive wonderfully....The orchard shows evidence of the result of intelligent care and attention—horticulture as it should be.*

Ripe plums and apricots would be dipped in lye water, then water, and laid out to dry on trays. R.O. Baldwin added fruit trees to his Osage Ranch orchards as the train arrived in 1891. Later, the Bishop Ranch was reputed to have the largest Bartlett pear orchards in the world.

Ripe prunes and apricots were processed then laid out on trays to dry in the sun. This is a 1914 photograph from the Kuss Ranch. *Museum of the San Ramon Valley.*

With this diverse and large production of fruits and nuts, storage sheds for the lug boxes, walnut sacks, and trays were needed. In 1924, when the electric train ended its service, Charles J. Wood bought the Danville freight station and transported the building to their ranch, using a wagon pulled by their Denby truck. It became one of their storage sheds.

Walnuts Everywhere

Alamo's Myron Hall is recognized as the father of the Bay Area's walnut industry. Don Wood wrote that Hall "grafted a Persian variety English walnut onto a native black walnut tree in 1873," producing an easily cracked, flavorful nut. His daughter Lucy Hall recalled her family all knocked the nuts down, getting together at the "time of nutting....Harvesting the walnuts was always a headache. You had to work long hours sorting and peeling off the hulls and getting your hands black and sorting out the bad ones."

Harvesting walnuts was done by hand, using a large pole to shake the limbs when the nuts were ripe, a laborious procedure which left people with aching necks. Travis Boone of San Ramon improved the process by mounting two or three towers on a tractor with which farmers could shake the trees. Later, power shakers did the job. Over the years, migrant workers

Poles were used to knock ripe walnuts off the trees and provided a literal pain in the neck. *Museum of the San Ramon Valley.*

picked up nuts for the large growers. There was a Filipino crew at Bishop Branch, "Gypsies" at the Boone Ranch in San Ramon, and Japanese and Mexican laborers at Baldwin Ranch.

Techniques for hulling and dehydrating the walnuts evolved from using the sun and drying them on trays to utilizing gas-fired dehydrators. Most large ranches had walnut processors, and others went to a grower-owned cooperative, the Contra Costa Walnut Growers' Association, in Walnut Creek until the 1950s.

In the twentieth century, the valley floor was covered with walnut and pear groves. Pears were ideal because they didn't ripen for a period after they were picked. By the 1920s, the acreage of walnut orchards exceeded those planted for fruit.

Agricultural Challenges

In order to have successful ranches, farmers began implementing pesticide applications in the 1910s, often delivered by high-pressure spray rigs pulled by horses. Don Wood described the chemicals:

> *Lead arsenate was used on pears and grapes, combinations of lime, copper and sulfur were used as sprays and dusts to control scale insects. Nicotene dust was applied to walnut to reduce blight and sulfur alone was applied to grapes and tomatoes to prevent fungus infections. After World War II DDT insecticide and 24D broadleaf herbicide were added to the chemical arsenal. These were applied using high-pressure spray rigs, then an air blast sprayer and other techniques.*

Aerial pest control was also used. Don Price, a dusters' pilot, flew a Stearman airplane out of the Bishop Ranch airstrip from the mid-1940s to the 1950s. The Stearman had two straight, noisy exhaust pipes. Farmers managed the walnut husk fly in the early 1970s, and black line disease limited the life of walnut trees to thirty or forty years. A disease called "pear decline" hit the orchards in the 1960s.

When the freeway opened in 1964, and new housing developments were built on the valley floor. The combination of homeowner worries over pesticide distribution and their lack of respect for private property, airplane noise, increased taxes, and decreased crop production contributed to ranches being sold throughout the valley. Ranches belonging to Baldwin, Meese, Wood, Wiedemann, Boone, and Bishop ended agricultural production. Many of these ranches had begun in the mid-1800s, with direct family descendants finally deciding to sell. A stubborn Armand Borel continued his family's small walnut grove into the twenty-first century.

In a 1990 interview, as the vast agricultural lands filled with new populations, Ann Wiedemann Kaplan said, "It is too bad that it is all being developed, but what can you do? It is a beautiful area with wonderful climate and you can't fault people for wanting to live here."

Commercial agriculture in the valley came to an end.

7

GETTING AROUND

Roads and Rails

Getting in and out of Danville in the late nineteenth century meant using the horsepower of actual horses on unpaved, potholed roads. Changes in transport gradually transformed valley life. In 1891, the Southern Pacific Railroad arrived with its many advantages, and from 1914 to 1924, an electric railway served the community. New bicycles, automobiles and trucks led to widespread efforts to improve roads by 1910.

Roads followed original Native paths adjacent to San Ramon Creek and elsewhere. They were initially named for their destinations. The first named road came after the Gold Rush and was called the Martinez to San José Road. If travelers went north, it was called the Martinez Road. If traveling east from Danville, people took Tassajara Road. Later, Diablo Street (now Road) led to Mount Diablo and the Mount Diablo Country Club. In 1892, the board of supervisors tried unsuccessfully to name the road from Martinez south to the county line Contra Costa Highway.

Dirt roads had choking dust in the summer and omnipresent mud in the winter, preventing easy crop and cattle transport, restricting family travel, and stunting growth. It took all day to transport products to Port Chicago or Port Costa, and the horses pounded the dirt into a stream. Stagecoaches did stop at Front Street periodically.

One *Contra Costa Gazette* article in 1890 reported, "Danville has lived almost alone for the last two weeks, there being very little travel on account of the bad roads in every direction after we get a few miles away from town."

The Danville Highway was lined with elm trees after the Great War. *Museum of the San Ramon Valley.*

San Ramon Branch Line of the Southern Pacific

Valley ranchers had been working to get a railroad for decades. The Southern Pacific was reluctant to build the north–south line through Contra Costa County that was envisioned by area leaders. In 1890, most farmers and landowners from Avon to San Ramon Line agreed to provide the land if the railroad would build a track and run the train.

Not everyone wanted the San Ramon Branch Line to cut through their ranches. A committee composed of August Hemme, Robert O. Baldwin, J.M. Stow, Albert Glass, and John A. Shuey was eager to welcome a train and met with reluctant landowners to get their support. This committee was set up to convince owners to agree to put the train in the right of way; some of them demanded compensation. Ultimately, funds were raised so the nay-sayers could be compensated and the right-of-way readied for the train. Sycamore Valley ranchers Charles Wood and David Sherburne donated substantial notes to help pay for the right-of-way.

In the summer of 1891, excitement swept the population as the train was completed. Newspapers waxed poetic.

The *Contra Costa Gazette*, on June 10, 1891, reported:

> *The beauty of the country seemed to increase as the train sped on.... Danville is reached in 2.20 miles. It is conveniently near the track, though measurably hidden by the trees. It is a thrifty locality with the modern tendency to progressiveness. The neat church is a conspicuous object from the track, and the sound of the church-going bell greeted the ear as a pause was made at this point.*

With the station in place, Danville's tiny village began to grow, just as boosters had hoped. In 1891, John Hartz laid out the Hartz addition, with new streets from the railroad station to Front Street, opening up additional possibilities. A boardwalk three planks wide was built from the depot to John A. Shuey's store and post office on Front Street.

New businesses provided accommodations and services to railroad passengers, as warehouses and corrals were constructed near the tracks. There were half-hour lines for teams hauling hay and grain to the new warehouses. Shuey's warehouse could store 3,500 tons of hay at a time.

The train opened up this section of central Contra Costa County for the timely shipping of farm products and movement of people, and ranchers planted more fruit crops since better transport was available. Rancher R.O. Baldwin added eight thousand new fruit trees to his Osage Ranch property.

The Danville Depot, in 1910, was one of Southern Pacific's classic decorative depots, identical to those in Concord, Walnut Creek and San Ramon. *Bancroft Library.*

After the steam train arrived in 1891, John Halverson built and operated the Halverson Liberty Stable, boarding horses and renting horses and buggies. *Museum of the San Ramon Valley.*

Soon, newspapers reported that Danville had as many buildings erected in three months as it had in the past thirty years. Halverson's Livery Stable allowed salesmen to rent horses or buggies for their visits to ranches, and the Danville Hotel and Mountain View Hotel served visitors beginning in the 1890s.

People used the train to visit friends, get to the county seat at Martinez, and shop. The very first year it opened, a delegation from Danville went to Martinez via rail to lobby the board of supervisors to vote against a liquor license sale, calling it "a menace to the well-being of the community."

As reported in the *Gazette* in 1891:

> *When the San Ramon train arrived Monday morning it brought a delegation of 70 strong from Danville, many of them ladies, and all of them among the best class of people of that neighborhood. Each wore a bit of blue ribbon conspicuously displayed and, on landing, marched up the street in couples.*

The reporter continued, "Danville is noted as the center of a prosperous, highly cultivated and progressive neighborhood, and the moral tone is exceptionally high."

These debates went on for decades and included a fight over the license of the Lawless Saloon, which later became Elliott's. A 1900 list of names petitioning for licenses included R.O. Baldwin, James Root, and Reverend R.S. Symington (against) and Fred L. Humburg, John Hartz, and W.C. Andreason (in favor).

The Danville Branch of the Electric Railway: 1914–1924

On September 3, 1913, the Oakland, Antioch and Eastern Railway (OA&E) opened its eighty-five-mile route from the Oakland ferry to Sacramento as a high-speed electric interurban railway. Just a year later, on March 2, 1914, the railway's Danville Branch arrived, linking Alamo and Danville to the outside world in a whole new way.

For a decade, the Danville Branch of the OA&E extended from Saranap (west of today's Rossmoor), over the hills near today's Crest Avenue, down Danville Boulevard, through Alamo and Danville, then east over the San Ramon Creek and fields to Robert Burgess's new Mount Diablo Park Club, a distance of 10.15 miles. Weekend electric trains that were run to promote the swank new club were dubbed "Million Dollar Specials" by the locals.

Nicknamed the "Toonerville Trolley," after a popular cartoon of the day by Fontaine Fox, the branch line was somewhat of a stepchild, with a recycled baggage car (Motor 1051) and eccentric conductor. Riders fondly gave it additional nicknames, such as the Alligator, the Dinky, and the Riveter.

Each day at Saranap, Motor 1051 was unbuckled from a larger train and sent to the valley. During the Great War, valley commuters went to the shipyards at Bay Point (Port Chicago) using the train. Paul Ogden said it took him fifteen minutes on the Dinky to get from Alamo to Saranap, where he boarded the regular train with hundreds of other people going to the shipyard.

Margaret and John Baldwin Jr. rode the train to dental appointments in Oakland and used it to return on weekends from the University of California, Berkeley. She recalled the train going over the Flournoy's open field east of downtown Danville. Wilson Close's uncle was a motorman on the electric line and Wilson remembered, "My uncle would take me on the engine, and I remember the excitement of riding in the locomotive."

This page, top: Danville Branch's electric train in downtown Danville. *Museum of the San Ramon Valley.*

This page, bottom: A billboard picture showing that Mount Diablo was accessible to travelers who used the electric railway. *Museum of the San Ramon Valley.*

Opposite: This view of Danville from 1914 shows (*left to right*) the Danville Hotel, a warehouse, the depot with a church steeple behind it, a warehouse and the Shuey house on School Street. *Museum of the San Ramon Valley.*

There were large protest meetings held when the abandonment of the train was proposed in 1923. The June 9, 1923 *Danville Grange Herald* asserted, "The beautiful settlement at Diablo depends upon it....[And] with a little expenditure for better facilities...the road could be made to pay well." The paper also linked a campaign to fund the new Mount Diablo State Park with the need to keep the electric train.

Nevertheless, in 1924, the branch line ended. Buses met each electric train in Walnut Creek, and a bus service appeared on the Danville Highway. The Toonerville Trolley was no more. The *Contra Costa Courier*, on February 29, 1924, commemorated the line's end with a droll little poem:

Toonerville, old Toonerville, we knew you well,
No more you'll battle through the dell,
No more your faults, to all, disclose.
At last you've earned a long repose.

For a decade, freight and passengers could choose between the electric and Southern Pacific's steam railroad—an excellent level of rail service. Efficient as the interurban service was and as popular as the Danville Branch was, ultimately, the automobile won out.

GOOD ROADS FOR THE NEW AUTOMOBILES

Enter the astonishing new automobiles and the trucks and tractors which revolutionized farming efficiency. The use of horses declined, although some horses were used regularly on valley ranches well into the 1930s. This decline also meant fewer workers were needed on ranches. Motorized vehicles revolutionized travel and transformed farm and ranch work.

Cars helped reduce "the differences in outlook between the farmer and the city dweller," said historian Walton Bean.

People remembered their first cars and often wouldn't buy any other brand. Taking the lead in 1911, John Baldwin Sr. bought a Cadillac, and Charles J. Wood purchased a Chalmers. George Wood said they also had the first truck in Sycamore Valley. As soon as he could reach the pedals around age twelve or thirteen, he was driving.

He recalled, "I'll never forget when ol' Charlie Goold saw that thing running down the road. He thought it was a runaway because it was going ten miles per hour. Teams never went more than two or three miles per hour." Since the dirt road was recessed from use, Goold could only see the top of the truck.

Oscar Olsson opened a gasoline and service station at the northeast corner of Diablo Street and Hartz Avenue, initially wheeling a portable gas pump out to serve cars. In 1919, he was the Overland car agent, advertising the Overland Roadster for $845 and contending its ride gave the driver a "smooth sailing sensation instead of bouncing and swaying."

Years later, in a *Tri-Valley News* interview, Hazel Wiester recalled when her husband bought his first car. He "bought from the only garageman in town." A 20 percent slope on a Danville hill became the testing ground for new automobiles. "If a car couldn't make it up the hill, no one would buy it."

Again, Grange Worthy Master Will Stewart took the lead, this time in pursuing better roads. In 1909, he called a meeting in Martinez, which initiated the first Good Roads League in Contra Costa County. Between 1910 and 1920, California voters approved $73 million for highway construction.

On July 22, 1919, a county bond issue for roads passed easily: Danville 182–1, Alamo 65–0, and Tassajara 58–1. An advertisement in the *Contra Costa Courier and Danville Journal* listed the bond's advantages:

1. *Because, good roads mean prosperity.*
2. *Because good roads mean an annual saving of thousands of dollars to the taxpayers.*

> 3. *Because, under the proposed bond issues, we get good roads now.*
> 4. *Because, unless the bond issue is voted the Supervisors must increase the tax rate or curtail the road building program. This would be a calamity.*
> 5. *Our industries demand good roads, farmers require them; taxpayers are willing to pay for them.*

One of the first paved roads in the county was built between Walnut Creek and Danville. A concrete highway extended from Martinez to Dublin by 1920. It was described in one booster newspaper as "a Beautiful Concrete Highway That Runs Through the Town."

Initially, the pavement ended abruptly south of town. Fay Tarlock wrote, "Motorists blissfully enjoying the smooth road, did not notice the sudden ending into the mud or dust, according to the season. The one garage in town had a jolly period of prosperity."

The center of this highway had a raised bump, about six inches high and fifteen inches wide, which was a real challenge to passing drivers. Ruth Boone said it was someone's goofy experiment that didn't work out. The bump was finally removed in 1930.

The tree-lined thoroughfare south and north of the village was attractive and made driving enjoyable. In 1935, a new state road system was created; State Route 21 extended from Walnut Creek to Mission San José.

A car park for campers was established on Front Street after the old Danville Grammar School was demolished in 1923. The *Danville Grange Herald* wrote:

> *The school lot together with our hall will soon present a cleaned up appearance and make a beautiful park suitable for picnics and other recreations. Danville should be proud to possess so fine and commodious a building as the fraternal and social hall, surrounded as it is by this nice park.*

Indeed, Californians loved their cars. A *Los Angeles Times* article in 1926 said it all: "Our forefathers…set forth 'the pursuit of happiness' as the inalienable right of mankind. And how can one pursue happiness by any swifter and surer means…than by use of the automobile?"

8

DANVILLE GROWS INTO ITS OWN

1870–1900

For decades after Inman sold land parcels to merchants, when people spoke about the "town," they meant the Danville area west of San Ramon Creek, at the intersection of Front and Diablo Streets. It was described in a *Contra Costa Gazette* article on March 26, 1887:

> *The make-up of Danville is about what you would find in most country towns. It has the usual number of stores, blacksmith shops, one saloon, two churches, Grange hall and school house, where there is a good public school maintained, and there is some talk of starting a high school.*

The San Ramon Creek gradually washed out buildings on the east side of Front Street. This included the original Cohen Store, according to one account by Charlotte Wood. A *Gazette* writer noted that one day, half of the street caved in and slid down into the San Ramon Creek. In 1887, the *Gazette* reported, "Mr. John Conway and Mr. James Close have been doing a good job of work in the creek opposite Conway's store; they have driven willow posts along the bank to prevent it caving off."

The Close property was in a central spot in Danville's downtown. James Close's first purchase in 1875 was that of Daniel Inman's original property. It included an acre of land at Diablo and Front Streets, with a house, a blacksmith shop, and a barn out back, all for $1,100 in gold coin. The old smithy was torn down and rebuilt with modern improvements early in 1892 and James Close operated the shop until he died in 1904. The Close General

Store on the corner of Front Street and Diablo Road had a second floor, which hosted the International Order of Odd Fellows Lodge (from 1892 to 1913) and the Neighbors of Woodcraft.

The hamlet was a sleepy place until Southern Pacific's San Ramon Branch Line was completed in 1891. Shortly after the railroad arrived, the *Gazette* reported:

> *Mr. John Hartz recently laid out a part of the town into blocks and lots as an addition to the town, on the south-west sides, and the town has spread in these directions, that is in the direction of the railroad depot, and so rapidly has it built up that it looks like a "brand new" town from the train or depot.*

This subdivision created Hartz Avenue and new east–west streets called Prospect, Church, and School Streets. The lots measured fifty by fifty feet and fifty by one hundred feet. Not long after Hartz subdivided his property, in 1895, Ralph Harrison submitted another development map for the area north of Diablo Street on what was formerly Sophia Love Boone's property.

Newspapers reported that the railroad promoted the village's growth and facilitated passenger activities, such as getting wedding licenses in Martinez, visiting friends in Concord, and shopping in San Francisco.

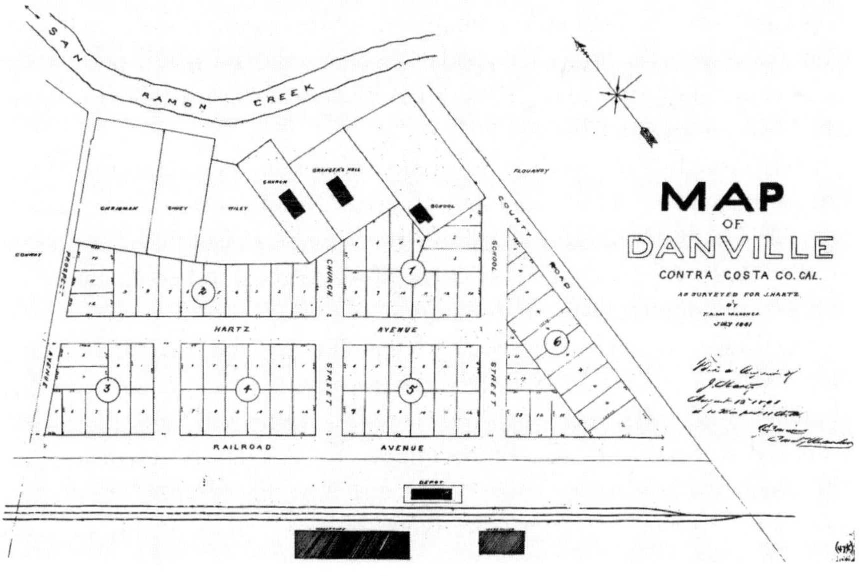

After the train station severed his ranchland, John Hartz developed the eastern part, submitting this map to the county in July 1891. *Museum of the San Ramon Valley.*

A drawing of the Danville Depot, Shuey house and warehouses. *Museum of the San Ramon Valley.*

The *Danville Sentinel* reported this news for a time, its byline stating, "On guard for the interests of the San Ramon Valley." In the 1890s, the energetic John Shuey ran a general store, owned warehouses by the depot, and served as postmaster.

Ina Boone Root, who grew up in the area (born in 1873), recalled the Noonan Saloon on the northern corner of Front and Diablo Streets, with commercial buildings constructed by James Close to the south. Over the years, three general stores along Front Street were owned by Cohen, Conway, and Close and were typical emporiums with barrels of pickles, salt, and beans. She said today's Prospect Avenue was "just a footpath then," which was nicknamed Tiger Alley.

Even though some businesses began to shift to Hartz Avenue, Front Street was still a center of community activity, with the Presbyterian church, Danville Grange Hall, and Danville Grammar School in place during the 1870s–90s. In 1898, Lawrence's new meat market on Prospect Avenue dealt in beef, pork, mutton, veal, and sausage.

The village was an ethnic stew similar to others in California. On Front and Hartz, the mixture included the first general store (Cohen, Jewish), the 1892 Danville Hotel (McCauleys, Irish), Peters and Freitas Big Store (Peters and Freitas, Portuguese), Danville Emporium (Foster, Portuguese), the blacksmith and stores on Front Street (Close, Canadian), A.M. Fitchenmueller's tin shop (German), a Chinese laundry, the bank (officers Numa Boone, Baldwin, from the East Coast) and Olsson's gas station (Olsson, Swedish).

This view of Front Street, circa 1915, shows three buildings owned by James Close. Notice the blacksmith in the middle and the International Order of Odd Fellows' second-floor meeting room. *Museum of the San Ramon Valley.*

Front Street, looking north, circa 1915. *From left to right*: Cohen's original store, Prospect Avenue, Joe McCeil's barbershop, the Conway store, the post office in a Close store, a blacksmith shop, and another Close store. *Museum of the San Ramon Valley.*

DIVERSIONS

In 1887, the Danville Grange No. 85 hosted an enormous harvest festival along Front Street at what was called Grange Park. Four to five hundred teams came from the East Bay, with an estimated 1,500 people, "to renew old and make new acquaintances; interchange the courtesies of our fraternity; to compare notes and stimulate thought and action by a few hours of recreation and social intercourse," according to a *Pacific Rural Press* article.

In 1898, Council No. 33 of the Portuguese Union of the State of California (UPEC) was established in Danville. The council provided business contacts and social events and helped pay funeral expenses. UPEC member 19 was Frank Noia, who owned a large ranch east of Danville that was later added to the Blackhawk Ranch. There, he and his wife, Mary, raised eleven children. Julia Noia recalled attending Green Valley Grammar School with her siblings, rain or shine. After she married Joseph Freitas, they lived at 439 Hartz Avenue in a house that is still standing; the family later moved to a ranch east of Danville.

FIRES UPSET EVERYTHING

Fires were terrifying facts of life for the San Ramon Valley pioneers. The long, dry summers and lack of water supply were enormous challenges to overcome when fires started. Volunteers fought with gunny sacks soaked with creek water and put water in leather buckets to douse the flames and then count on the wind to change. Sometimes, the buckets were called "chimney savers," since chimneys were usually the only parts of buildings to survive fires.

In 1887, a devastating fire on Wood Ranch in the Sycamore Valley swept the entire wheat crop away just as it was ready to harvest. The ranch expected three thousand sacks of grain but harvested only thirty, and it had no insurance. Charlotte Wood wrote, "Father was in San Francisco and Brother Louis on his way home from Davis with our header to cut the grain, but when the two reached home that evening, three black hills met their gaze instead of the six-foot-tall waving grain."

The *Contra Costa Gazette* covered another conflagration in July 1891:

> *We have had considerable excitement this week. The hot weather has dried grass so thoroughly that the least spark makes a roaring flame in a very few*

Pioneer men at Cox's grove, circa 1890. *Left to right*: Albert W. Glass, Joe Lewis, Milton Larabee, William Meese, Levi Maxcy, Edward McCauley, Samuel Ramage, Lee Parker, Edward Shuey, Albert Stone, Samuel More, Charles Goold, John Chrisman, Myron Hall, David Glass, William Z. Stone, Nathaniel Howard, Robert O. Baldwin, James Boone, William Cox, George McCamley, and Elisha Harlan. *Museum of the San Ramon Valley.*

> *seconds. On Monday everyone was called out by generous impulse to fight a fire in Mrs. Flournoy's place near Danville. A hundred men or more rushed immediately to put it out with wet sacks and plows, but the field (a crop of chevalier barley) was strewn with bundles of heavy grain and six inches of barley leaves lay all over the ground, so it was useless to try to stop it until the wind turned and blew the flames back.*

The Flournoys were large landowners and possessed the land east of Old Town and San Ramon Creek. The *Contra Costa Gazette*, on December 19, 1896, reported, "Mr. John Flournoy is building a thousand dollar bridge across San Ramon creek opposite Mrs. Laura Flournoy's homestead, cost of which he is giving to his mother as a Christmas present." Today, there is a walking bridge near this location.

Temperance Activities

For decades, groups were concerned about alcohol consumption nationally and in California. San Francisco was the largest city in the West and prided itself on providing hospitality to one and all. Saloon owners actively opposed the temperance movement.

Several organizations opposed liquor consumption, including the Sons of Temperance, the Good Templars, the Woman's Christian Temperance Union, and the Anti-Saloon League. The columns of the *Contra Costa Gazette* tell about the efforts of the "drys" to convert the "wets" beginning in the nineteenth century. In the 1870s, communities could vote on local liquor option sales, and even though they could not vote, women were active in these campaigns.

Issues of liquor licensing in Danville were well covered in the *Gazette*, which, on February 10, 1900, reported, "The Saloon Fight—Two of Danville Cases Heard Last Tuesday." A "spy of the anti-saloon league" brought charges against the bartender of A. Flagel. Justice W.C. Lewis heard the case in Danville; forty witnesses were summoned, and the paper said:

> *The town was livelier than it had been for many a day....It seems the County supervisors felt that, since liquor had been sold there for many years, it was better that "the men have retail licenses when they are under bond to keep the law."...The result is that Danville will become a wide-open town.*

Danville had its share of strong temperance supporters. What we call substance abuse today was known as "demon rum" then. Temperance groups, along with many others, carried the temperance banner in California

R.O. and Mary Baldwin's new house was built in 1888. The local *Gazette* wrote that it was "a ten thousand dollar house on the modern plan, which will be an ornament to our valley." *Museum of the San Ramon Valley.*

and the nation, with the Eighteenth Amendment to the U.S. Constitution the result.

Danville businesses served the productive agrarian community. R.O. Baldwin wrote in the March 26, 1887 *Contra Costa Gazette*:

> *I will name a few of the fruits that are best adapted to this valley, although we raise more or less of all kinds; apples, pears, prunes, all kinds of plums, and figs, and many kinds of berries; also various kinds of nuts; the almond is especially well adapted and is a sure crop, and pays well, and there is no rush to harvest or market the crop.*

The valley ranchers also produced wheat, barley and hay while cattle continued to graze on the hills. In the next century, walnut and pear orchards predominated. By 1900, an estimated two thousand people lived in the San Ramon Valley.

9

THE TWENTIETH CENTURY

1900–1930

Danville in 1900 was the largest community in the San Ramon Valley, with a lively railroad station located next to the village. There were about four hundred people in town. On April 18, 1906, the San Francisco earthquake and fire marked the start of the century for the entire Bay Area.

There were many stories of that early morning earthquake. Most Danville chimneys were damaged, including John Chrisman's at 169 Front Street, the Mountain View Hotel's on Hartz Avenue, and the Baldwin house's south of town. China fell off the shelves all over the valley. Soon, San Francsico's conflagration lit up the western sky.

Vivian Coats of Tassajara Valley later wrote:

> *Chickens were squawking, cattle bawling and the neighbors' dogs were howling. In the pantry the pans of milk, set to let the cream rise, were on the floor along with broken glasses and some broken dishes....The square brick chimney on the roof cracked around evenly and made a half-turn.... As the day wore on the western sky was red and then black with smoke from burning San Francisco.*

John Vecki and his family came to Danville from San Francisco after the quake and moved into the Chrisman house on Front Street, putting his dental office in one corner. Nearby were the Close properties, where a substantial family home was built in 1898 on Diablo Street. The Close family hosted popular church ice cream socials each year.

Built in 1866 for the Cohen family, this house was bought by the Veckis after they fled the 1906 San Francisco fire. Standing in front of it are *(from left to right)* Mary Allen (Claire's mother), Claire, Victor, and Isabel (Victor's mother), with children Victor Jan and Isabel. *Museum of the San Ramon Valley.*

With Hartz Avenue available, the center of town gradually moved there. Elliott's Bar, M.J. Medina's Danville Shoe Store, Lawrence's Meat Market on Prospect Avenue, the Danville Emporium, McDonald's Drug Store, and the Danville Shaving Parlor were popular. The Danville Hotel shifted to Hartz Avenue from Railroad Avenue in 1927.

Close's general store (later Acree's), the brick San Ramon Valley Bank (1908), and the American Legion Hall (1925) were located on the corners of Prospect and Hartz Avenues at the center of town. Joe A. Freitas and Frank Peters used the same brick design as the bank and built The Big Store around it, with entrances on Hartz and Prospect Avenues. A two-cell jail (mostly a drunk tank) was located on Hartz Avenue, with constables in charge. On Front Street, the Presbyterian church and a new Fraternal and Social Hall were important destinations.

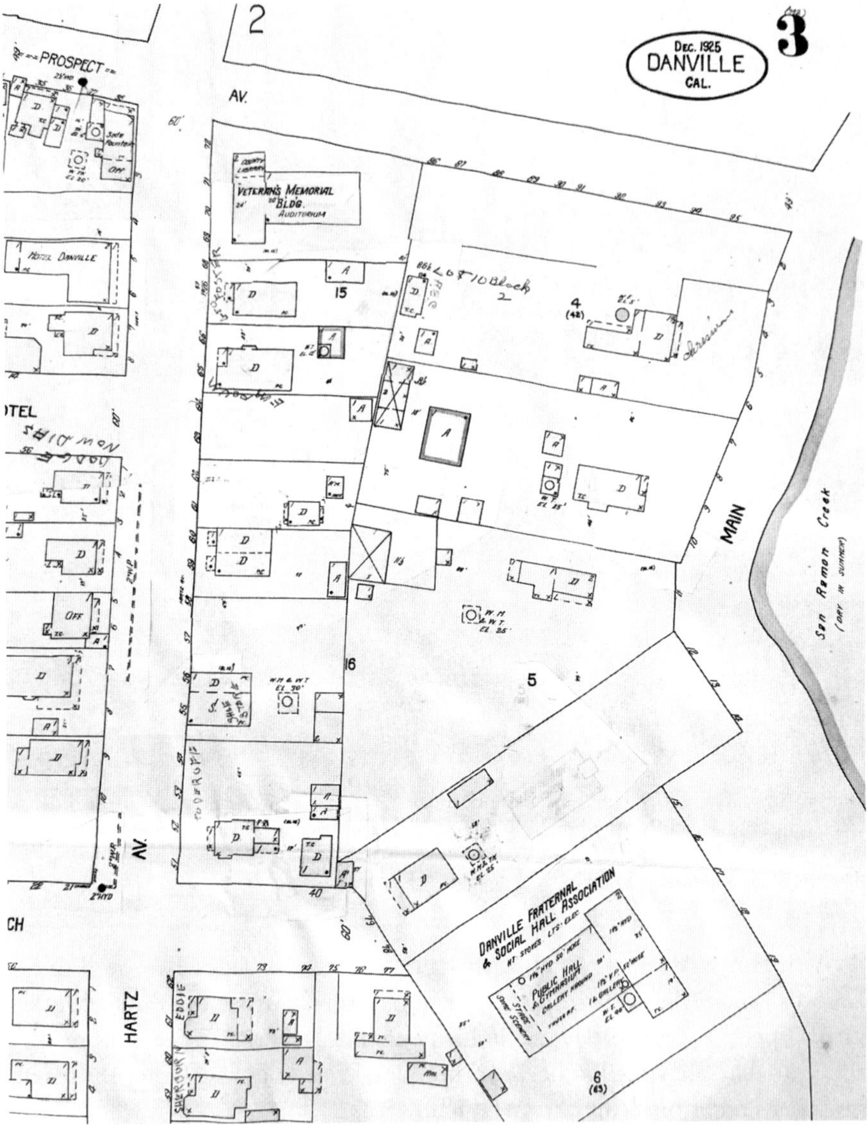

Above: This Sanborn Insurance map (1925) shows the new American Legion Hall at the top, stores and houses and the Presbyterian church and the Fraternal and Social Hall in the lower right-hand corner. *Museum of the San Ramon Valley.*

Opposite, top: The Danville Improvement Club stationery logo, circa 1925, shows the names of the officers and board of directors, with a heart inscribed "Danville in the Heart of the San Ramon Valley." *Museum of the San Ramon Valley.*

Opposite, bottom: The handsome brick San Ramon Valley Bank at Prospect and Hartz Avenues is shown here with the electric railway tracks, circa 1920. Notice the wooden sidewalks, horses and cars. *Museum of the San Ramon Valley.*

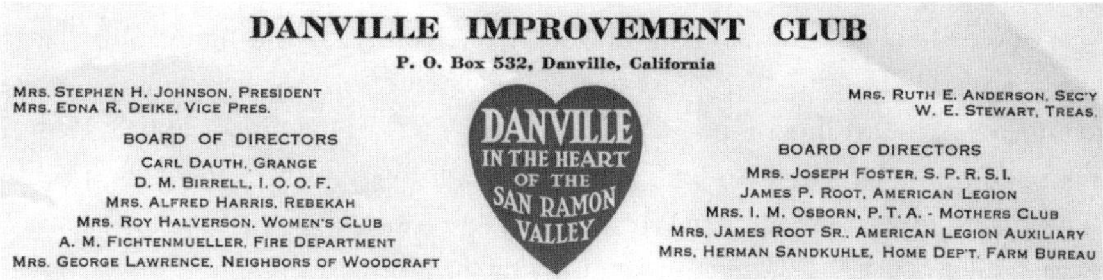
DANVILLE IMPROVEMENT CLUB

P. O. Box 532, Danville, California

Mrs. Stephen H. Johnson, President
Mrs. Edna R. Deike, Vice Pres.

BOARD OF DIRECTORS
Carl Dauth, Grange
D. M. Birrell, I. O. O. F.
Mrs. Alfred Harris, Rebekah
Mrs. Roy Halverson, Women's Club
A. M. Fichtenmueller, Fire Department
Mrs. George Lawrence, Neighbors of Woodcraft

DANVILLE IN THE HEART OF THE SAN RAMON VALLEY

Mrs. Ruth E. Anderson, Sec'y
W. E. Stewart, Treas.

BOARD OF DIRECTORS
Mrs. Joseph Foster, S. P. R. S. I.
James P. Root, American Legion
Mrs. I. M. Osborn, P. T. A. - Mothers Club
Mrs. James Root Sr., American Legion Auxiliary
Mrs. Herman Sandkuhle, Home Dep't. Farm Bureau

In 1911, at Hartz and Linda Mesa Avenues, St. Isidore Catholic Church was completed and became the center of a large parish. Built with fine pine and other high-quality materials, the unique church was built by many locals who were proud of it. Joe and Laura Wilcox Fereira were the first couple to be married there.

The many Danville organizations included the Grange, Odd Fellows, Neighbors of Woodcraft, Good Roads League, and a Portuguese Union of the State of California chapter. Beginning as a Danville Grammar School Mothers' Club in 1911, the Danville Women's Club soon looked farther afield, becoming the San Ramon Valley Welfare Club and finally the Danville Women's Club. In 1911, the Danville Improvement Club, with Lillian Close as president, announced its motto: "Make Danville an Ideal Hometown.

A *Danville Grange Herald* newspaper was printed in 1923 and 1924 at the Wood Ranch printing shop by George Wood and Bertha Mariano. The *Danville Grange Herald* featured Danville happenings, with articles on the proposed Mount Diablo State Park and the electric train's demise.

Not far from Danville, the new 1914 Mount Diablo Park Club was established and made a huge impact. There were jobs for residents and the excitement of "Million Dollar Special" electric trains, which came through Danville between 1914 and 1924. In 1917, club developer Robert Burgess sold 1,250 acres in the south Mount Diablo foothills to Ansel Mills Easton, who built a home designed by architect Christian Mullgardt, raised Shire horses and Shorthorn cattle, and named the property Blackhawk Ranch.

DANVILLE'S BRANCH LIBRARY

While a small traveling library from California's State Library came to the Grange in 1906, 1913 marked the first physical library in town. Then on November 9, 1913, the Danville branch of new county library opened with 104 books. These were placed in the Danville Improvement Club room over the post office in one of the two-story Close buildings on Front Street.

Three women shared the librarian duties: Ellen Ainslie (the wife of the Presbyterian minister), Lillian Close (from the Danville Improvement Club), and Phoebe Halverson (the owner of a local beauty salon). Others who helped were Elma Galvin and Mrs. J. Higley.

In 1926, the library moved to a corner room in the new American Legion Hall. Edith Clark was appointed librarian in 1925 and served for twenty-five years. Patrons could also use a stereo viewer to look at slides from all over the world.

WOMEN WIN THE VOTE IN 1911

An election on October 10, 1911, stirred people up, since California's ballot included the proposal for women's suffrage and three progressive direct voting powers—the initiative, recall, and referendum. The Danville Grange sponsored a public meeting on the franchise issue. Its August minutes recorded: "It was planned to have a debate at our next meeting and upon the subject—Resolved 'that Women be granted the right of suffrage.' Affirmative Sister Nina Williams and S.E. Wood—negative Bro W.E. Stewart."

Energetic Bay Area women campaigned for the franchise, and several attended this Grange meeting. The College Equal Suffrage League brought its seven-seated Packard touring car, the "Blue Liner," which drew men to see the car and hear the "Votes for Women" message.

At the meeting, the *Contra Cost Gazette* reported, "A rising vote was called for from all people present…and the ladies were given the decision. There was a large crowd present from the surrounding country." That same day, a Danville Equal Suffrage Club was organized to support the vote, with officers Lillian Close, Libbie Wood, Nina Williams, and Ada Cornwall. All the Grange debaters (pro and con) joined the club.

Women narrowly won the vote in California. In Contra Costa County, the suffrage vote was 1,569 in favor to 1,548 against. However, in Danville, the men opposed the franchise for women 72 to 23.

A New Fraternal and Social Hall

After much discussion about the community's need for such a building, Grangers (who met at the 1874 Grange Hall) and Odd Fellows (who rented a space upstairs in a Close building on Front Street) agreed to construct a new fraternal and social hall. Plans were made, and the Grange Hall was hoisted to become the second floor. In no time, this hall became the place to meet and party when it opened in late 1913.

When the new high school was completed in 1917, boys would jog down the street after school to play basketball in the hall. Gordon Elliott recalled that court space was tight, and the players had to shoot baskets through the rafters, providing an unusual challenge for visiting teams.

In 1923, a movie was shown, advertised as the first of many "high-class films" to be presented at the hall. Duane Elliott said the curtain would close and show local business advertisements when there was a break to change the movie reels. At one point, during weekends, the hall was a roller-skating rink.

Finally, a Local High School

For forty years after the Union Academy burned down, students went to high school in Oakland or Berkeley, where they boarded and came home for weekends. Not all students went beyond the eight grades of grammar schools.

A view of Church Street, looking east, 1912. On the right are two Eddy houses with a barn. One house was the first high school from 1910 to 1914, located just behind the Danville Grange Hall. *Museum of the San Ramon Valley.*

A Grange-appointed committee, with members Charles J. Wood, Rev. J.G. Anderson, C.E. Howard, John F. Baldwin Sr., and S.F. Ramage, set out to organize a public high school. They reported that a high school district could be created if there were 200 students. In the valley's six grammar schools (Danville, Alamo, Green Valley, Sycamore, San Ramon, and Tassajara) there were approximately 452 students. If all were included in the new district, a net tax rate of $0.15 on each $100 of assessments would sustain the school district.

In 1910, a successful election (omitting Tassajara, which joined in 1920) supported such a district. The first board of trustees met on March 31; Baldwin was elected president, and the other members were Charles J. Wood, William Meese, A.H. Cope, and David Bell. Will Stewart was secretary.

The new San Ramon Valley Union High School opened in 1910 with Theadore A. Cutting as principal and teacher Miss Ada Cornwall. At first, they met in a vacant house belonging to the Eddy family. near the Grange on Church Street. A curriculum of six courses was offered: commercial, history, English, German, mathematics, and physical geography.

Writing about opening day, the *Gazette* stated, "Thirty-five students have already enrolled and many are expected to enroll within a short time. This is one of the most important steps that has taken place in Danville for some time."

The classes met there until 1914 and then moved to the newly vacant Odd Fellows' second-floor space on Front Street. Work on a new school proceeded, and finally, in May 1917, classes moved to the Mission-style school north of Danville, designed by architect Norman R. Coulter of San Francisco.

New Inventions Enliven Danville

Electric wires were extended to Danville in 1911 and to the depot in 1913. These wires enabled the Danville Branch of the electric railway to operate from 1914 to 1924. By 1927, wires were extended to ranches in Sycamore Valley. George Wood recalled that Wood Ranch had two thirty-two-volt power generators, which ran on gasoline and were started by hand. His family had indoor lighting and bought some new electric appliances, including a vacuum cleaner and a toaster.

A telephone trunk line extended from Martinez to San Ramon's Bishop Ranch by 1900. Telephone operator Viola Root said there were fifty-seven

The valley telephone operator Viola Root is shown at the telephone exchange, located on Hartz Avenue. She was the operator from 1917 to 1952, when dial phones were introduced. *Museum of the San Ramon Valley.*

valley subscribers in 1915 and one hundred in 1920. Her first switchboard was located just south of Elliott's Bar on Hartz Avenue. Farmer lines with eight to ten subscribers per line stretched out from downtown Danville. Clients paid twenty-five cents a month or three dollars a year to join and had to make repairs to their own line—and all listened in.

Change was in the air. In the 1920s, women would come into Phoebe Halverson's Phyllis Beauty Shop on Hartz Avenue with long hair down to their waists. "After it was bobbed, they almost all went into a crying jag for a time," said writer Virgie V. Jones.

A New Fire District

The long, dry summers, periodic strong winds and lack of water supply were enormous challenges when fires started. In 1912, the Danville Improvement Club created the Danville Farm Defense Fire District. Their first equipment included a trailer equipped with ten ten-gallon milk cans full of water and gunny sacks.

The Danville Fire Station expanded to two bays in the village center. Notice the siren behind the building. *Museum of the San Ramon Valley.*

Then the Danville Fire Protection District (DFPD) was created on September 6, 1921. After some lively boundary discussions, the district's area came to include the Alamo, Danville, Sycamore, and Green Valley Grammar School Districts, plus Elmer Baldwin's ranch, a region of about fifty square miles.

On March 18, 1922, William Ward, John Jones, and Joe Freitas were elected fire commissioners. In April, they bought a Reo-American La France 45 chemical fire truck for $4,140, which was stored at the Olssons' downtown garage. Constable Oscar Olsson was made fire chief. Telephone operator Viola Root was responsible for sounding the siren near the 1925 station.

In October 1925, a Mount Diablo fire nearly destroyed the state park's tollhouse, reached the upper part of Diablo Park Club, and threatened Danville. Chief Albert M. Fichtenmueller was burned around his face and hands as three hundred men fought the fire. In 1926, a fire destroyed the Danville Emporium and adjacent buildings.

The Great War

Although a war had raged in Europe since 1914, Americans were resolved to stay out of it. Viola Lynch's high school graduation valedictory address in 1914 supported the peace movement.

After the United States joined the fray in April 1917, the first local boys left for the military. Most trained at Camp Lewis, near Tacoma, Washington. The high school yearbook, *The Valley Kernel*, published the names of all the boys in the military. Five of them died: Simeon Anderson, Peter Beyer Jr., George Freitas, William Peterson, and Lloyd Wood.

Liberty bonds were sold, and in 1918, Danville had 290 subscribers for a total of $37,100 and received an honor flag. The town's volunteer salesmen included Charles J. Wood, Theodore Nissen, John F. Baldwin Sr., Al Wiester, and chairman Frank A. Marshall. Women knitted scarves and socks for the Liberty Boys, just in time for their trek to the European winter.

Competing with the war for headlines, a devastating influenza outbreak began in 1918. Probably starting in a Kansas military camp, the epidemic's total American fatalities were an estimated 500,000. Masks were required as bars, churches, lodges, and schools were closed down for a time.

When the Armistice was signed on November 11, 1918, everyone rejoiced. A young George Wood recalled everybody running up and down the street, dragging cans. "People were ready to celebrate."

PROHIBITION

The country's temperance advocates were finally victorious when Prohibition went in effect in 1920 and closed the valley's legal saloons. Elliott's Bar (then called the Eagle Bar) had thrived for nearly two decades. With Prohibition, County Sheriff R.R. Veale told owner Hiram Elliott that, since he was such a good citizen, Veale would ignore his liquor sales out the back door but couldn't protect him from federal enforcers. Elliott decided to close the saloon, in part because he didn't think violating the law was a good example for his sons. On January 17, 1920, drinks were on the house, and the family broke all the liquor bottles, according to Elliott's son Duane.

The saloon became the Danville Ice Cream Parlor, which advertised National Ice Cream and a full assortment of candies and tobacco, phone 34-J.

People continued drinking, whether it was legal or not. The 1920s were famous for stills in remote areas of Crow, Norris, and Cull Canyons, where Italian and Portuguese entrepreneurs produced a popular drink called Jackass brandy.

The 1914 *Contra Costa Courier and Danville Journal* praised the valley:

> *Never did the San Ramon Valley present a more attractive appearance than now, and in the past it has always been pronounced one of the most beautiful spots of earth. The balmy spring air is laden with the perfume of thousands of fruit blossoms and the green hills with the growing grain in the rich valley are delightful to look on.*

10

LET'S PARTY!

Parties and "red-letter days" were welcome parts of Danville life. Ranch work was unrelenting and get-togethers were anticipated happily, whether they were spelling bees at the grammar schools, potlucks, dances, barbecues, or July Fourth celebrations. The Grange Hall was the center of things beginning in 1874.

The *Contra Costa Gazette*, on March 17, 1891, reported:

> *The young people met at Grange Hall last Saturday evening and organized a Social Club. Any one can become a member on application. There will be literature, music, games and dancing, as may seem best from time to time.*

Vivian Coats Edmonston recalled good times in Danville as she grew up and attended Sycamore School and the new high school. She said, for youth, there were trees to climb, coal mine entrances to explore, horses to ride, and games to play. Then there were picnics, church socials, Grange and Odd Fellows dinners, family gatherings, and just "visiting around." "Who said country life was isolated and lonely?" said Vivian.

Picnics

The closing ceremonies at Green Valley School in 1893 provide a glimpse into nineteenth-century party times. The *Gazette* reported that there were

Top: Around 1890, this family group was at Cox's grove, probably for a picnic. *Left to right, first row*: Ella Peterson, Ella Coats, Loreta Glass, James Coats, Minnie Harlan, Mabel Harlan, and Carrie Ledden. *Left to right, second row*: Ida Hall, unidentified, unidentified, Elisha Harlan, Mira More, Laura More, Lilly Glass, Albert Glass, Kate Howard, Jennie Baldwin, Helena Hemme, Ed Shuey, Lillie Elliott, Mary More, Samuel Ramage, and Jim Ramage. *Museum of the San Ramon Valley.*

Bottom: The entrance to Woodside Farm shows a barn with a cupola in the background, circa 1894. *Wood family archives.*

drawings on the blackboards, floral offerings, and flags. Under the supervision of teacher Kate Howard, there was singing, recitations, dialogues, marches, and drills. The paper commented that parents owed much to Miss Howard for "the moral as well as the intellectual welfare of their children." Then all enjoyed a "sumptuous repast" and "a picnic of ye old times."

Lucy Hall remembered many picnics but noted one in particular.

> *One picnic…I want to tell you about was one at the Woods. They had a fire which destroyed four hills of wheat, their whole year of produce, and had no insurance. People from all over the Valley brought loads and loads of food and grain to help them out. My grandfather was the first to appear with a load of grain, according to George Wood. Each year the Woods had a picnic to thank people in the Valley to show how gratified they were.*

Charlotte Wood often hosted themed parties at Woodside Ranch in the Sycamore Valley. In 1912, the following advertisement went out: "Living Pictures, An out-of-door Entertainment for the benefit of the Danville Grange will be given at 'WOODSIDE' Saturday evening, Sept. 28 at 8 o'clock. Admission 25 c. Refreshments 10 c."

Families packed picnic lunches with any excuse, going on day trips to Mount Diablo, long excursions to Yosemite, and visits to friends out of the area.

Ramona Park

A picnic grounds at Ramona Park was popular for decades, especially in the spring. In 1906, on a section of his ranch four miles south of Danville, William Meese built a picnic area which took advantage of its proximity to the new railroad and San Ramon Creek. Several promotions touted the ten-acre tree-covered Ramona Park, which had a picturesque little lake, large shade trees, a dance pavilion, and a ball field. Picnicking, swimming, boating, baseball, dancing, and rowing were all popular parts of the park.

Because temperance principles were to be followed in the park and within two miles of the premises, women and children were assured "perfect freedom from the insults," according to the *Martinez Daily Gazette* from April 18, 1906.

A flyer announcing the 1906 opening of Ramona Park on the Meese property. *Museum of the San Ramon Valley.*

The park's opening was delayed because of the huge San Francisco earthquake and fire on April 18. When it did open on July 4, 25 percent of the receipts for the day were sent to the earthquake relief committee by the International Order of Odd Fellows Lodge No. 378, which organized the day. The IOOF grand master gave a traditional Independence Day address. On opening day, a special train left San Francisco at 8:00 a.m. and returned at 5:00 p.m.

Locals enjoyed the area as well. In 1912, a high school basket picnic was scheduled for Ramona Park. The *Gazette* wrote, "At this season of the year a more beautiful spot can't be found." After the high school opened in 1917, the park's grounds were often used for student events, since Meese was on the school board.

Later, other buildings where events and parties could be enjoyed were opened, including the 1911 San Ramon Hall, the 1914 Fraternal and Social Hall on Front Street, and the 1925 American Legion Hall at Prospect and Hartz Avenues.

July Fourth Fêtes

Patriotic July Fourth celebrations were regular, anticipated annual events. In the nineteenth century, patriotic speeches were given, followed by games, ample picnics, and fireworks lighting up the valley.

In the 1850s, one Danville celebration came with a beef and mutton barbecue, blackberry pie, and oranges to taste. Interspersed with band numbers, Daniel Inman and John M. Jones gave speeches. And on July 4, 1854, Jimmy Smith recited "Patrick Henry's Address Before the Virginia Convention" by memory and received ten dollars for the feat.

A July Fourth celebration north of town in 1864 included the usual food, games, and speeches, but tensions between Democrats and Republicans bubbled over. Later, James Smith recorded what happened that day. During the Civil War, many valley people were "states' rights" Democrats, including Danville founders Dan and Andrew Inman.

Smith recalled that one family, the Crows, were "known to have very decided political opinions, strongly Republican." The Crow boys were Jep, Granville, John, Francis, and William. They were probably a pretty hardy crew, enjoying the break from ranch work with everybody else.

According to Smith:

> *Finis Johnson, the preacher's son, had memorized the Declaration of Independence and began to recite. He got a short way into the speech, probably reaching "governments are instituted among Men, deriving their just power from the consent of the governed…" when objections rang out.…One of the Crow family arose and in forceful language asserted, "No secession speech shall be delivered here!" And followed with stronger language.*

A photograph of a July Fourth parade featuring Danville's 125th Anniversary. *Museum of the San Ramon Valley.*

> *Great excitement at once prevailed. Women screamed. All the Crows flocked together and for a short time there was great excitement that resulted in the meeting being broke up. Families rushed to their conveyances and started for their homes.*

Smith did not record whether young Finis was rewarded for his memory work.

Independence Day celebrations were grand after World War II ended in 1945. During one 1949 party (with games, speeches, dances, and food), the Lions and American Legion had a good-spirited game of tug of war. In 1951, one barbecue at the high school hosted 650 people.

Today's version of the July Fourth parade and community parties began in 1962, after enthusiasm for Danville's September Hay Days events began to fade. Virginia Deaton, Liz De Chene, and Casey LaFortune wanted a patriotic celebration appropriate for families. At the high school, they organized a parade, children's games, hot dog stands, a patriotic talk from a military officer, and fireworks. It became a template for Independence Day events for the next sixty years.

DANCES

In the late 1800s, people came from all over to dance at the grammar schools, parking babies on quilts or blankets in the cloak rooms. These were all-night affairs, with people driving home at sunrise to do morning chores.

The *Walnut Kernel*, in 1941, wrote:

> *What is probably the oldest continuous series of dances in Contra Costa county is conducted monthly in the Danville veterans' hall by the Mt. Diablo Post of the American Legion. On the first Saturday of the month the post and women's auxiliary have an old-time dance where middle-aged folk may enjoy the polka, schottische, mazurka, Danish polka, waltz, two-step, quadrille, lancers and other dances they learned as children.*

Hazel Wiester recalled these dances, where a favorite orchestra came from Livermore and people arrived from all over. "We would dance to midnight and have a substantial dinner, then go back and dance some more....My first dance was at the San Ramon Hall, which a women's club took care of. Always there was a 'big feed' at midnight, with chicken, potato salad, pies."

She and Ed Wiester went in a horse and buggy, "which was the beginning of my courtship."

During the Great War, in April 1918, a large encampment of high school cadets camped in Green Valley, according to the *Contra Costa Gazette*. One evening, the "cadets gave a band concert, parade and drill from 6:30 to 8 o'clock, after which they went to the Social hall and held an informal dance." Fifteen cents was charged for admission, and ice cream cones were sold, with profits going to the Red Cross.

Portuguese families would get together for parties with music and food. Both Joseph Freitas Sr. and Joseph Freitas Jr. were talented musicians and played a violin, which the elder brought with him when he emigrated from the Azores in the 1870s. Joseph Jr. organized a band, with his friend Duane Elliott playing the guitar.

Other Diversions

Hunting was a favorite pastime—initially, bear hunting. It was a favorite sport and a necessary one while bears were still in the valley. Fay Tarlock wrote that the "old trails on Mount Diablo were the scenes of by-gone hunts. The grandmother of Wanda Goold was awakened one morning to find a bear in her kitchen making a quick breakfast of bacon and sugar." In later years, people hunted deer on Las Trampas, Mount Diablo, and in the valley.

The *Valley Pioneer*, on August 19, 1948, showed a photograph with the following caption: "Pete Camacho bagged a 132 pound deer in the Las Trampas Mountains on Sunday morning. In the photo are Peter, Chucky Fereira and his father Lee Fereira and Dean Springer." Olivia's Variety Store advertised red hats for deer hunters.

The San Ramon Valley Union High School—the only high school in the area from 1910 to 1965—had sporting events that brought people together. With only 104 students in 1933, the school was lucky to have 11 players plus a few on the bench. Its 1935 track and football teams were extraordinary.

Lee Fereira recalled:

> *We were fortunate then because we had a lot of really good athletes, all around the same time. Heck, our starting backfield in football was also our relay team. When we had a home* [football] *game on Friday afternoons everyone closed up their business to come and watch us play.*

Horseshoe champion Guy Zimmerman pitching a horseshoe in the Danville Hotel courtyard, circa 1955. *Museum of the San Ramon Valley.*

Local plumber Guy Zimmerman was the California men's horseshoe champion from 1942 to 1948 and an international champion in 1954. That year, Montair School's *Blue Paper* newsletter reported:

> *The big celebration for Guy Zimmerman will be held this Sun. on the grounds of St. Isidore's Church. There will be a parade, free beer, cokes, hot dogs and turkey sandwiches plus an exhibition by the champ himself. Admiral Chester Nimitz, avid horseshoe enthusiast will be there....*Life *and* Time *magazine representatives along with metropolitan newspaper reporters will also be there.*

During the 1940s, the newspaper listed Whist parties held by the Rebekahs, the Neighbors of Woodcraft, St. Isidore's Guild, and the Alamo, Danville, and San Ramon Mothers' Clubs. Other card parties were held all the time.

Distance runs for good causes and special parades enlivened the community. Nancy Lewis and Jacquie Graham organized first Devil Mountain Run on May 21, 1978. This 10-kilometer (6.2 mile) "romp through the streets of Danville" benefited Rowan Branch of Children's Hospital. In 1978, the San Ramon Valley Little League All-Stars baseball

Art for a commemorative plate, which featured Mount Diablo, O'Neill's Tao House, the Old Oak Tree, and the Danville Hotel Restaurant and Saloon, 1984. *Artist, Virginia DeFreitas, Museum of the San Ramon Valley.*

team won the American Little League Championship in Williamsport, Pennsylvania. To celebrate, there was a Danville parade and an Emilio Deli's dinner for nine hundred people at the high school. Primo's to Primo's Run for Education began in 1984.

The town council led a year-long celebration of Danville's 125th birthday in 1983–34, calling it a "Silver Centennial." There were student history essays, a Danville poem read by teacher Al Gentile, a display of Hap Magee's ranching memorabilia in two large trailers, and a talk on Grange history by historian Inez Butz. The Alamo-Danville Soroptimists created a new Danville history quilt.

A commemorative plate was produced, which featured a painting by artist Virginia DeFreitas. And a stunning coffee table book, *Danville: A Portrait of 125 Years*, was created by Marillyn Cozine, Roz Hirsch, Pauline Weber, Sylvia Kennett, Jean Cuff, and Barbara Hubinger.

Hundreds came to Railroad Avenue for a unique depot-moving event on June 6, 1996. That Sunday, the 1891 Southern Pacific Danville Depot was shifted from its location 810 feet north to the southwest corner of West Prospect and Railroad Avenues. The street was closed, tracks were chalked on the street, and a parade featured 4-H clubs and music. The depot was moved in one piece by Lopez Movers. In the parking lot, there were square dancers, demonstrations of small ranch gas machines, a band, and much conversation. Three years later, the depot was opened as the Museum of the San Ramon Valley.

Twenty-first-century events and gatherings continue to bring the community together. In 2008, the Hay Days event was revived during Danville's 150th celebration. There are car shows, Hartz Avenue festivals, street runs with concluding parties, and Armistice and 9/11 events. And always, there's the signature July Fourth parade and lighting of the Old Danville Oak Tree.

11

YEARS OF CHALLENGE

1930–1945

By 1940, the community had an estimated 1,225 residents, with 2,120 in the entire valley. Danville's small downtown included a post office, a saloon, grocery stores, gas stations, a drugstore, a barbershop, a telephone exchange, a post office, a five and dime store, a meat market, an ice cream parlor, and a shoe store. Curtis Haskell (constable of the Danville Judicial District from 1944 to 1958) ran Haskell's Plumbing and Hardware Store from 1927 to 1944. Edwin Olsson's gasoline station was located at the corner of Hartz Avenue and Diablo Road.

The 1930s in Danville

Fay Tarlock described Danville in the 1930s:

> *One of the oldest communities in the west, the locality has retained much of pristine charm and beauty. Here life has a fair meaning. The air is pure and clean as it was intended to be when the world was created.…Everything that grows from the earth grows better in Danville. Here the climate is genial, tempered, mild, delightful! Danville, most favored of the Cyclops mountain. All that Diablo has to give, it gives first and most abundantly to Danville: scenery, climate, soil, location.*

McDonald's Drug Store on Hartz Avenue was built in 1922 for $10,000. In 1958, it became Randall's Pharmacy, and a decade later, it was Bill's Danville Pharmacy. *Museum of the San Ramon Valley.*

At 210 Front Street, the classic Danville Presbyterian Church burned down during a ferocious windstorm in 1932. The next year, parishioners rebuilt it in a California mission style. It stood next to the Fraternal and Social Hall, which was destined to become the Village Theatre.

Also on Front Street, an open space area was informally called the Grange Park and included the area where the nineteenth-century Danville Grammar School once stood. A new Danville Elementary School had been built in 1922, close to San Ramon Valley High. Just southwest of the park, near School Street, Fukuchi's Japanese grocery store and school were in place. Japanese American students met there on weekends, where they learned to speak Japanese and understand Japanese culture.

During the Depression years of the 1930s, ranchers suffered, and some ranches were foreclosed. George Wood said, "A lot of people came from Missouri and Oklahoma. All they had was their car, and they didn't have any money. We didn't either." Lois Kamp Gompertz recalled "hobos" carrying all they owned on their backs and coming by her father's dairy on Blackhawk Road. Her mother would feed them in exchange for chopping some firewood.

Orchards like this one covered the valley floor for most of the twentieth century. *Museum of the San Ramon Valley.*

Mount Diablo State Park

Public access to the summit of Mount Diablo and the state park opened in 1931, after years of effort by Grangers Charles J. and George Wood, the Danville Women's Club, the Sierra Club, and many others. A five-hundred-car parade, organized by Sheriff R.R. Veale, began in Martinez and drove over rose petals the Sunset Nursery spread over Highway 21.

When heavy rain and lightning halted the parade at Diablo Country Club, dignitaries stopped for libations. Rose Ferreira recalled that the governor was "drunk as a skunk and it took two men to hold him up." Finally, a mellow Governor James Rolph Jr. cut the ribbon not far from the club and opened what the *Contra Costa Gazette* called "the road leading to the celestial Contra Costa County peak."

Having Fun in the 1930s

Also opening in the 1930s were the new Bay Bridge (1936), the Broadway Low Level (later, the Caldecott) Tunnel through the hills to Oakland (1937), and the Golden Gate Bridge (1937). Historians mark the Broadway Tunnel and Bay Bridge openings as the end of Contra Costa's isolation from the rest of the San Francisco Bay Area.

When the Broadway Low Level Tunnel opened in 1937, these high school girls attended. *Left to right:* Joanne Miles, Barbara Conklin, Florence Symmons, and Mildred Lewis. *Museum of the San Ramon Valley.*

In 1939–40, the Golden Gate International Exposition on Treasure Island drew visitors from Danville, California and around the globe. Young people bought season tickets and went every weekend. If you were eighteen, you could visit Sally Rand's Nude Ranch. During Conta Costa County's two special days on September 17, 1939, and September 22, 1940, samples of agricultural products sold or given away included almonds, walnuts, celery, fruits, cider, grapes, and onions.

In the late 1930s, an experienced chef, Paul Zeibig, leased the Danville Hotel, obtained a liquor license, and proceeded to provide fine dining. Patrons came from great distances to enjoy a dinner out in Danville. People remembered him walking downtown with his chef's hat on. The war, with its gas rationing, ended that business, although he made some effort to continue at war's end.

Lew Tromp was the only high school coach from 1933 to 1944 and recalled the origin of the football field. When he arrived and asked about the field, the principal, Joe Bissig, went over to a window facing Las Trampas Ridge and said, "There it is." Later, Tromp said, "I'll never forget it. There in front of me was a field all right, but it was filled with a tangle of milkweed and thistle four feet high." He hired a farmer to disk the field about five times.

"We started playing on it, and the boys ground it down with their cleats." Both the San Ramon Valley team and the field were hard on visiting athletes.

Lee Fereira, Ted Main, Eldred Ramos, and Bob Frick were hometown heroes, recognized for their track achievements and football success. Fereira said that in 1935, Frick posted a 9.6-second time in the one-hundred-yard dash, a feat which was only .2 seconds off Jesse Owen's one-hundred-yard Olympic gold medal record of 9.4 seconds in 1936.

Orphans from San Francisco continued to stay at sunny Camp Swain during the summers, arriving by bus, walking into town for ice cream, and generally enlivening the area. The year 1941 marked their last visit, and in 1946, the Magee family bought the camp property.

Newspapers featured various organizations started by Danville leaders. Several helped establish the Contra Costa County Development Association in 1937. After having been a member of the state Cattlemen's Association for twenty years, Charles J. Wood was the prime mover in creating the Contra Costa–Alameda Cattlemen's Association in 1945. The Lions Club began in 1940, with a revitalized Danville Chamber starting in 1949.

World War II

The attack on Pearl Harbor on December 7, 1941, shocked everyone. Pete Camacho recalled that everyone asked, "Where the hell is Pearl Harbor?" He and his five brothers soon enlisted and went to war; his family hung a flag with six blue stars at their home.

As America declared war against Japan, Germany, and Italy, war fever swept the country, with concerns about the Japanese, German, and Italian immigrants who lived here. Italian families who lived near the San Francisco Bay were told to move away from the water, and their loyalty was questioned. One man pointed out that they couldn't penalize Italian immigrants, as that would force baseball star Joe DiMaggio's mother to move.

With the attack, Japanese American families reflected the face of the enemy. Young Ace Handa recalled, "We were all mad at Japan for bombing Pearl Harbor and scared, too." Instead of focusing on possible spies and using due process of law, all Japanese citizens, including Japanese Americans, were targeted. Federal Order 9066, in May 1942, sent all Japanese Americans who lived on the West Coast to internment camps "for their own safety." Today, this is acknowledged as a disgraceful, racist decision that displaced 120,000 people.

Japanese American families from the valley departed from the Danville Depot with only their suitcases; they were sent first to the Turlock Fairgrounds to live in barracks and then to the Gila River Internment Camp in the Arizona desert.

Phil (Choji) Ajari grew up in Danville and served in the South Pacific as a Japanese translator, always with a white soldier by his side. *Museum of the San Ramon Valley.*

One family's story is typical. The Ajari family grew pears and tomatoes just north of the high school on Danville Boulevard. The father, Eddie Ajari, was taken from his home with no warning a week after Pearl Harbor. The family's four American sons had varying war experiences. Jun Ajari was a pharmacist and had gone to Japan for additional schooling; he was returning home on December 7 when his ship turned back. In Japan, he was jailed and then forced to fight in the Philippines.

Phil (Choji) joined the U.S. Army and served as a Japanese language interpreter in the South Pacific. Hideo Ajari was a farmer in Colorado and stayed there, since farming was considered an essential occupation. The youngest, Charles, graduated high school in 1941 and was interned with the family in Gila River. He was critical about the entire experience, even though he registered for the draft. Later, he said, "I was mad, frustrated and upset....Here we were, born in America and then put behind barbed wire and guards with machine guns."

Three Japanese American boys from the valley served in the decorated 100th/442nd Regiment, Ace Handa, Kats Hikido, and Tom Sakata. This regiment suffered the most casualties of any American regiment. When Hikido's legs were shattered by a landmine, he was hospitalized for over two years and, after seven operations, he was able to walk again. On the GI Bill, he attended Stanford University.

During World War II, everyone coped with gas and sugar rationing and planted victory gardens. Penicillin was used broadly for the first time, with dramatic results. Locally, Don Wood recalled, "Schools closed for a week

Pete Camacho, Lee Fereira, and Gordon Elliott, pictured in front of Elliott's Bar in 1944. *Chuck Fereira.*

in late September and encouraged students to pick walnuts." Those who picked stood out because, for weeks, their hands were stained dark brown by the walnut hulls.

East of Danville, the Civilian Conservation Corps had previously constructed a camp at the corner of Tassajara and Blackhawk Roads, which became Camp San Ramon. There, Army troops underwent fitness training and schooling. Later, the camp became an Italian war prisoner site, with opera songs drifting across the valley.

When the war ended in 1945, Danville and the valley began to grow and change. Soldiers had come through California on their way to the South Pacific and liked what they saw. By the late 1940s, the weekly *Valley Pioneer* reported, "New residents are coming in at the rate of a family a day."

At the important Danville intersection of Hartz Avenue and Diablo Road, a census reported 3,700 vehicles passing north and south in January 1934. By 1949, that number was nearly 16,000. While the Rancho El Rio subdivision had offered lots for small ranches by San Ramon Creek beginning in the 1930s, the explosive growth began soon after the war.

Hartz Avenue was a quiet little street before the war. But as the population grew, the Root and Boone houses north of town were moved and replaced by gas stations. Rose Ferreira, who lived on Rose Street (not named for her), recalled thirteen or fourteen gasoline stations along Hartz Avenue and Danville Boulevard, with people nicknaming the area "gasoline alley."

Danville reflected the country after the war ended: young families grew and crowded schools, a variety of jobs were available throughout the state, minorities were prevented from buying homes, and the birth control pill was still in the future.

In a talk to the Danville Women's Club in 1945, Charlotte Wood said, "Attracted by the salubrious climate, the beautiful orchards and hills and views of Mount Diablo, numerous home seekers have chosen to locate in the vicinity of our pretty little village of Danville. We welcome them kindly and wish them well."

12

EUGENE O'NEILL IN DANVILLE

In 1937, a couple moved to Danville's western hills and put the town on the map. American playwright Eugene O'Neill and his wife, Carlotta, using funds from his Nobel Prize for Literature, built a secluded home and called it Tao House. The O'Neills were one of the most famous couples in the country, often appearing in magazines and newspapers. Eugene was on the front of *Time* magazine on October 21, 1946.

Sinclair Lewis summarized the playwright's accomplishments in 1930:

> *O'Neill has done nothing much in the American drama save to transform it utterly in ten or twelve years from a false world of neat and competent trickery to a world of splendor, fear and greatness.*

Eugene and Carlotta Monterey were married in 1929, Eugene's third and Carlotta's fourth marriage. By that time, Eugene had written three Pulitzer Prize–winning plays and was the country's most renowned and innovative modern playwright. His well-known early plays include *Anna Christie*, *Desire Under the Elms*, and *Ah, Wilderness!* His drama *Mourning Becomes Electra*, based on a Greek tragedy, was produced in 1931.

In 1936, O'Neill was awarded the Nobel Prize for Literature, the first and only American playwright to receive this recognition. At the time, the couple had moved to Seattle, where reporters and well-meaning invitations besieged them. Carlotta's daughter Cynthia drove the O'Neills to the San Francisco Bay Area, as they considered settling there.

Carlotta had grown up in Oakland, where, as the former Hazel Tharsing, she had been Miss California and later became an actress, renamed Carlotta Monterey. O'Neill needed peace and quiet to write. At the age of forty-eight, after a dissolute youth that included bouts of tuberculosis and alcoholism, he was in poor health and needed easy access to medical care. Carlotta was determined to provide such a place and had created other homes for Eugene, including a renovated château in France and the palatial Casa Genotta in Georgia.

Eugene O'Neill's portrait appeared on this postage stamp in 1967. *Public domain.*

A Final Home and Harbor

They searched for a new home in the San Francisco Bay Area, bought 158 acres in Danville's Las Trampas Hills and built Tao House. As a reflection of Eugene's interest in Oriental philosophy and Carlotta's love of all things Asian, Tao House was designed using a combination of Chinese and California ranch motifs. It had a view of the iconic Mount Diablo and was set in lovely natural surroundings with mild weather and plenty of privacy. Their full staff of six included Herbert Freeman, who was their driver, friend, and man of all work.

Eugene and Carlotta Monterey O'Neill, with Tao House and the valley behind them. *Eugene O'Neill Foundation, Tao House.*

O'Neill wrote to his friend Kenneth Macgowan about Tao House: "It is absolutely country…without a taint of suburbia…yet only three-quarters of an hour motor ride from Frisco." In another letter, he wrote, "We have a beautiful site in the hills of the San Ramon Valley with one of the most beautiful views I've ever seen. This is the final home and harbor for me. I love California. Moreover, the climate is one I know I can work and keep healthy in. Coastal Georgia was no place for me."

O'Neill usually worked in the mornings, had a late lunch, and then walked in the adjacent Las Trampas Hills. He used the swimming pool regularly, though it was no real substitute for the Atlantic Ocean swimming he had once relished. He called the place his "rancho," and he pored through catalogues and bought a variety of chickens, all which were named. One favorite was a belligerent roster called Sugar Ray Robinson.

Blemie Remembered

Blemie, the couple's Dalmatian, was loved by Eugene and Carlotta. Sometimes, the dog would wander, and their neighbors would call the house. Freeman (who was not a great fan of the dog) was sent to retrieve him.

When Blemie's end was near, in 1940, O'Neill wrote a touching tribute to help console Carlotta. Part of this tribute could have served as Eugene's own epitaph. The following is an excerpt:

> *The Last Will and Testament of an Extremely Distinguished Dog*
>
> *I, Silverdene Emblem O'Neill (familiarly known to my family, friends and acquaintances as Blemie), because the burden of my years is heavy upon me, and I realize the end of my life is near, do hereby bury my last will and testament in the mind of my Master....*
>
> *I ask my Master and Mistress to remember me always, but not to grieve for me too long. In my life I have tried to be a comfort to them in time of sorrow, and a reason for added joy in their happiness. It is painful for me to think that even in death I should cause them pain....*
>
> *I suggest a Dalmatian as my successor. He can hardly be as well bred, or as well mannered or as distinguished and handsome as I was in my prime. My Master and Mistress must not ask the impossible. But he will do his best, I am sure, and even his inevitable defects will help by comparison to keep my memory green. To him I bequeath my collar and leash and my overcoat and raincoat, made to order in 1929 at Hermès in Paris. He can never wear them with the distinction I did, walking around the Place Vendôme, or later along Park Avenue, all eyes fixed on me in admiration.... Here on the ranch, he may prove himself quite worthy of comparison, in*

Left: O'Neill and his beloved Dalmatian Blemie. *Eugene O'Neill Foundation, Tao House.*

Opposite, top: Tao House in 1939. *Eugene O'Neill Foundation, Tao House.*

Opposite, bottom: O'Neill at his desk on the second floor of Tao House, where he wrote his final plays. *Eugene O'Neill Foundation, Tao House.*

some respects. He will, I presume, come closer to jackrabbits than I have been able to in recent years. And, for all his faults, I hereby wish him the happiness I know will be his in my old home.

One last word of farewell, Dear Master and Mistress. Whenever you visit my grave, say to yourselves with regret but also with happiness in your hearts at the remembrance of my long happy life with you: "Here lies one who loved us and whom we loved." No matter how deep my sleep I shall hear you, and not all the power of death can keep my spirit from wagging a grateful tail.

But peace, at least, is certain. Peace and long rest for weary old heart and head and limbs, and eternal sleep in the earth I have loved so well. Perhaps, after all, this is best.

Life at Tao House

In 1939, the O'Neills' friend Miguel Covarrubias painted famous murals for the Treasure Island Fair in San Francisco Bay, not far from Danville. He and his photographer wife, Rosa, visited the O'Neills at least twice. Rosa took one photograph of a smiling O'Neill at his player piano, Rosie. Miguel drew a caricature of Carlotta while they were there, just as he'd drawn one of Eugene in New York during the 1920s.

Eugene and Carlotta O'Neill, drawn by artist Miguel Covarrubias in the 1920s and 1939, respectively. Covarrubias drew murals at the Treasure Island Exposition. *Eugene O'Neill Foundation, Tao House.*

With only one guest bedroom, the O'Neills had relatively few visitors. O'Neill had been an absentee father to his three children, but his son Eugene O'Neill Jr. came four times. His second son, Shane, was their first overnight guest, and his daughter, Oona, visited twice. When Oona turned eighteen and married famed actor Charlie Chaplin (age fifty-four), O'Neill never spoke to her again.

O'Neill needed complete silence to write, and his plays written at Tao House addressed not only the human condition but also his family's adversities. Sometimes, he was overcome with emotions as he wrote. Carlotta religiously kept people away so he could work. As the "keeper of the gate," she was often called the Dragon Lady by critics for this devotion.

And work O'Neill did. At Tao House, he completed five of his most significant works: *A Moon for the Misbegotten*, *The Iceman Cometh*, *Hughie*, *A Touch of the Poet*, and *Long Day's Journey into Night*. He also wrote *More Stately Mansions*, a manuscript discovered later.

The O'Neills had lived in France in the 1920s and tearfully followed World War II battles in Europe on a large map. As Freeman and other staff members left for war jobs and military service, the O'Neills were helped by several local Danville people.

Eugene wrote, "We have always liked these people…and evidently they have liked us, for they have shown a kindness money cannot buy and gone out of their way to help us." Later, Curtis Haskell said, "I went up [to bring a delivery from his store], and we started talking and became friends." Haskell helped the O'Neills with chores, drove them to doctors' appointments and brought them his wife's special clam chowder. Garage owner Edwin Olsson drove them as well.

One friend, Barrett Clark, wrote that this new interaction was important, since it "somehow helped restore the man's essential faith in a world which his reading and contemplation had, in a way, distorted."

The Eugene O'Neill National Historic Site

In 1944, the O'Neills sold their property to the Carlson family, who made some minor changes to the house and added nine hundred acres to the property to create a working ranch. They called their property the Corduroy Hills Ranch, using O'Neill's name for the hills. Park advocate Manfred Lindner wrote, "The real crown jewel is the Corduroy Hills, called the Carlson Ranch. It included a beautiful part of the [Las Trampas] ridge and canyons."

The house and property changed hands several times, and in 1968, plans for a housing development using Tao House as a community center were publicized. Outraged by this proposal, a determined trio of Danville-area women, Thalia Brewer, Darlene Blair, and Lois Sizoo, spearheaded a community movement to save the house and core property. In 1974, they created a nonprofit called The Eugene O'Neill Foundation, Tao House.

That same year, the East Bay Regional Park District supported this effort when it purchased 1,018 acres for Las Trampas Regional Wilderness, which included Tao House. A survey by the park district's Hulet Hornbeck enabled an appraisal of the 14-acre core property and house. The district gave the foundation an eighteen-month purchase option.

Actor Jason Robards, the O'Neillian actor of his generation, helped raise funds for the house with profits from performances of O'Neill's play *Hughie*.

Assemblyman Dan Boatwright successfully pursued Collier Emergency Park Funding, which enabled the house to be purchased by the State of California. In 1975–76, Congressman George Miller spearheaded legislation to create the Eugene O'Neill National Historic Site; President Gerald Ford

Above: Actor Jason Robards flanked by foundation members Loiz Sizoo and Darlene Blair. They testified before a Senate committee to save Tao House and the property as a National Historic Site. Senator Alan Cranston cosponsored the successful legislation. *Eugene O'Neill Foundation, Tao House.*

Opposite: "The Veil," part of the O'Neill Commemorative Project on Front Street, provides a quotation from his play *Long Day's Journey into Night. Artist Michael Manwaring; Eugene O'Neill Foundation, Tao House.*

signed it into law in 1976. The state deeded the site and house to the federal government in 1980. Now owned and managed by the National Park Service, the home was opened to the public in 1985. Litigation by the neighbors delayed full access until the case was settled in 1994. Regular performances at the site began in 1995.

The National Park Service partners with the foundation, which produces plays, provides educational programs, manages an artist in residence program, and sponsors an annual Eugene O'Neill Festival in Danville. The festival includes live performances, seminars, programs, history walks, and periodic O'Neill exhibits at the Museum of the San Ramon Valley.

LIKE A
SAINT'S VISION
OF BEATITUDE
LIKE THE VEIL OF THINGS
AS THEY SEEM
DRAWN BACK BY
AN UNSEEN HAND,
FOR A SECOND
YOU SEE –
AND SEEING THE SECRET,
ARE THE SECRET.
FOR A SECOND
THERE IS MEANING!
THEN THE HAND
LETS THE VEIL FALL
AND YOU ARE
ALONE, LOST
IN THE FOG AGAIN,
AND YOU STUMBLE ON
TOWARD NOWHERE
FOR NO GOOD REASON!

In 2017, a Friendship City relationship between New Ross, Ireland (from which O'Neill's immigrant Irish father departed), and Danville began with a theme, "One Festival, Two Countries."

An O'Neill Commemorative Project was created along Front Street in 2005 by artist Michael Manwaring, featuring the plays O'Neill wrote at Tao House and a quotation from *Long Day's Journey into Night*, titled "The Veil." It was supported by donors at a cost of nearly $130,000. This tribute to the playwright is located across from the Danville Library, Community Center and Green on Front Street and provides another reason to walk around Danville's Old Town.

When the O'Neills sold their ranch in 1944, Eugene wrote, "We've put the rancho up for sale. Too much of a burden and worry. It has us licked." And Carlotta stated, "We stayed at Tao House for six whole years, longer than we lived anywhere else. Of course, there were many hardships, but it was a beautiful place and I hated to leave."

After departing from Danville, O'Neill never wrote another play.

13

A VILLAGE TRANSFORMED

1945–1960

With World War II's end, the San Ramon Valley began to grow. No longer an exotic, unknown location, California became the place to be for good weather, jobs, and unlimited opportunities, which drew people from throughout the country. In 1950, Danville had 2,905 residents (doubled from 1940), and in 1960, it had 3,585. In July 1956, 27,000 vehicles a day passed through Hartz Avenue at Diablo Road.

Fay Tarlock, in the *Valley Pioneer*'s centennial edition, observed:

> *Then came the summer of 1948 when the first subdivisions were started. The friendly effervescence of the Valley went to newcomers' heads. They were in a town where they could belong to anything or everything. And the sky was their limit. Like many other expatriates from cities, they captured the schools, supplanting old time officials with their own candidates. For a few years school elections were more hotly contested than national ones. One election for Fire Commissioner, both candidates, bar owners, brought out the greatest vote Danville has ever known.*

The *Valley Pioneer* weekly newspaper began on February 2, 1945, and was a treasure-trove of Danville news, advertisements, and reports on social life. Growth and how to address it was often a topic. For example, the August 1, 1946 *Pioneer* reported that the San Ramon Valley Improvement Association was reviewing land use permits and developments proposed by the county.

THE VALLEY PIONEER

The Only Newspaper Published in and for California's Beautiful San Ramon Valley

Volume II | Thursday, September 12, 1946 | Number 33

Top: The masthead for the *Valley Pioneer*, a weekly newspaper that was published by Eugene Haney and C.C. Morse. *Museum of the San Ramon Valley.*

Bottom, left: Editor Beverlee Holly with her son Ernie in early 1945. Her husband was "somewhere in Belgium" at the time. *Museum of the San Ramon Valley.*

Bottom, right: John F. Baldwin Jr., the grandson of Danville pioneers R.O. and Mary Baldwin. He was the area's congressman from 1955 to 1966. *Museum of the San Ramon Valley.*

Beverlee Holly was the *Pioneer*'s first editor. She lived with her son in the back of the first *Pioneer* office (formerly the Lawrence Meat Market on East Prospect) and put little Ernie in a playpen by the front window while she worked.

There were many groups and clubs, old and new, with meetings and photographs covered in the *Pioneer.* The Alamo Lodge of Masons, Woodmen of the World, Lions Club, Alamona chapter of the Eastern Star, and several improvement clubs were only a few of the groups that were active in the community. In 1949, *Pioneer* articles regularly covered San Ramon Valley Town Hall meetings, which represented the interests of twenty-five large and small organizations in the valley and discussed current topics.

St. Isidore Catholic Church at the corner of Hartz and Linda Mesa Avenues was renovated in 1951. The brown shingles were moved and replaced with white fire-proof asbestos shingles and a new assembly hall was added in the rear. Father Thomas Collins pointed out that there were 30 worshipers in 1911 and 611 in 1951.

At 233 Front Street, the Fraternal and Social Hall was used by Grange, Odd Fellows and Rebekah Lodge No. 123 for four decades. Different events took place in the building: sport competitions, meetings, parties, dances, and live theater performances. In 1948, the hall became a movie house called the Village Theatre, which showed new movies every three days. The proprietors were Heaton and Marge Randall, whose cat often landed on unsuspecting laps.

In the 1950s, the original San Ramon Valley Union High mission-style school building was taken down over safety concerns. And in 1953, the Grangers moved to a new hall on Diablo Road land donated by Will Stewart. That same decade, the San Ramon Chapel (a mortuary) was established by Mel Whalen on Front Street.

Congressman John F. Baldwin Jr.

Congressman John F. Baldwin Jr. represented the San Ramon Valley (and beyond) for over a decade. After serving in World War II, he set up a law practice in Martinez with his eye on Congress. A Republican in a Democratic district, he lost his first campaign. He competed a second time, won, and served from 1955 to 1966.

Baldwin was brilliant, energetic and esteemed for his congressional accomplishments. He brought the Veterans' Hospital to Martinez, influenced the alignment of I-680, and established the John Muir National Historic Site. After his death from cancer in 1966, hundreds of people came to his memorial service. His name now appears on John F. Baldwin Jr. Elementary School and the Carquinez Strait Deepwater Channel.

HOME BUILDING ACCELERATES

Suburban growth was on people's minds. In the *Pioneer*, Fay Tarlock wrote about the decade between 1948 and 1958:

> *Beyond the village perimeter are the subdivisions, born of the past ten years. They are Danville Gardens, Montego, Danville Estates, Cameo Acres, Vista Grande, San Ramon Heights—to mention a few. With their built-in electric kitchens, patios, swimming pools and two-car garages, they are symbols of our time. Above them all is Montair of the oleander hedges, cool breezes, and California ranch-type mansions, bigger swimming pools and bigger vistas.*

Even though there weren't many San Ramon Valley jobs after World War II, people with an eye to the future thought that the valley would be a prime place for homes. And they were right. Homes were built at an ever-accelerating pace beginning in the late 1940s and as the I-680 Freeway was completed to Danville in 1964. Planned unit developments with smaller lots and shared community amenities became part of the changing face of the valley. Traditional wells and septic tanks were no longer adequate for this growth.

In addition to the ready market for homes, other factors contributed to the rapid conversion from agricultural lands to growing suburbs. Tax policy meant land was reassessed at a higher value. Cannery closings, the expense of replacing aging walnut trees, and a lack of interest in ranching by the younger generation all figured in the change.

In 1946, George Jovick bought 350 acres of the former Macomber Ranch in Danville to create the custom-built Montair Homes community. The houses were touted as being "country homes surrounded by the scenic beauty of oak knolled hills, mountains and valleys with water from the California Water Company....Protective restrictions, utilities and sites starting at $4,500." These restrictions were designed to prevent non-white races from purchasing homes.

According to Secretary Patricia Offield, Jovick and a local man established the roads for Montair by riding horses up the hill several times—quite different from future methods.

East of Green Valley Road, Cameo Acres was developed with one-quarter- to one-third-acre lots. Model homes were provided, which was a new approach for the valley. In 1951, three-bedroom homes with brick

Above: Riding her horse, Pat Offield looks across the rural valley to Mount Diablo from the Montair Homes property on Danville's west side. *Museum of the San Ramon Valley.*

Left: This Cameo Acres flyer advertised suburban homes selected from models, with special breaks for veterans. *Museum of the San Ramon Valley.*

fireplaces, copper plumbing, two wall furnaces, and cedar shingle roofs sold for $9,350. Veterans could put $50 down, pay $50 for closing costs, and own a house for $67 a month. Their water came from California Water Company; the Southern Public Utility District set up a sewer plant to serve the subdivision.

Residents of the Diablo Country Club were upset because the homes and the wastewater plant were built nearby. Unfortunately, the plant functioned poorly and smelled. Then a settling pond failed and leaked onto one of the Diablo golf holes.

There were some very unhappy people. Cameo petitioned to get sewer service from the Central Contra Costa Sanitary District (CCCSD). This effort precipitated much debate throughout the area because Danville and Alamo had voted down efforts to bring such pipes to the valley in an effort to forestall growth.

When County Health Officer Dr. H.L. Blum was tasked with addressing these sewage issues, he looked farther afield. He reported to the supervisors that 17 percent of the Alamo and Danville septic tanks were deficient and that better sewer service was "a necessary health measure." In 1955, the supervisors allowed CCCSD to create Local Improvement District No. 30 and place a thirty-inch line through Alamo and Danville with a smaller line extending to Cameo Acres and Diablo.

Flooding in several new housing tracts brought County Flood Control staff to Danville to discuss the problem. Las Lomitas, San Ramon Heights, Vista Grande, and the Hopper tracts were damaged during the winter of 1950–51. Ditches were built and drop structures and riprap were constructed at pivotal spots in San Ramon Creek.

Part of the valley was served by the California Water Company. Alamo Oaks celebrated when it received California Water Service in 1949, but water was still supplied by wells and springs in most areas. In 1958, voters in the San Ramon Valley Water District annexed to East Bay Municipal Utility District for their Sierra water, 3,084 yes to 127 no.

DANVILLE BEGINS TO CHANGE

Old Town Danville began to expand in this period. Some of the area's small businesses were Elliott's bar, Xavier's Shoes, Loard's Ice Cream and Candies, Olivia's Variety Store, Acree's grocery store, Turner's

Hardware Store, P-X Market, and Danville Warehouse and Lumber. Vally Medlyn's, named for its owner, opened in 1950. Austin and Elizabeth Root ran Root's Bar and Restaurant from 1943 to the 1960s across from the Veterans Memorial Building. The handsome Close family house (1898) was demolished in 1955 to make room for the twelve-thousand-square-foot Varsity Market on Diablo Road.

New and expanded services began to appear. Postmistress Ruby Podva announced that Danville's first rural delivery route would begin on August 1, 1945, although people still gathered at the post office to use their mail boxes. She served from 1933 to 1963, first at an office on Hartz Avenue and then at new buildings on East Prospect Avenue. In 1996, the post office moved to its present town location at Danville Square. Milk was delivered to Alamo and Danville residences by Williams Dairy until 1974.

In 1952, farmers' communal telephone lines ended. Operator Viola Scott Root pointed out there were 566 stations and 959 subscribers in the valley with over 500 people waiting for telephones that year. Pacific Telephone and Telegraph installed dial phones on January 6, 1952 at 12:01 a.m.

The new 1946 Danville Post Office at 169 East Prospect Avenue, with Diablo Postmaster Helen Cooper and Danville Postmaster Ruby Podva. *Museum of the San Ramon Valley.*

At the library in the Veterans Memorial Building, Myrtle Osborn was the librarian in 1945 and stayed on as an assistant to librarian Grace Warren in 1956. Young Winky Camacho worked part time at this library beginning in 1956 and said it was a tiny room with storage in the bathroom. The San Ramon Valley Library League successfully lobbied for a new library. When it opened in Danville on June 12, 1961, the San Ramon Valley Public Library was described as having a "space age" design.

Some father-son Saturday outings included visits to local watering holes. Chuck Fereira recalls going with his father, Lee, to Root's and the Shady Way Inn on Danville Boulevard, consuming soft drinks and hard-boiled eggs. Jim Feia took his son Alan with him on similar visits. Men talked with their friends over a drink, relaxed, and caught up on the news.

Hay Days celebrations were held in the fall for several years beginning in 1958 with a celebration of Danville's one hundredth birthday. Boosters promoted Danville for its "Old Century Leisure, New Century Convenience" and worked to draw customers into town.

One well-remembered event on September 4, 1957, was the arrival of Elvis Presley and his friends, who ate substantial breakfasts at Rex's Drive-In

Veterans dressed up for the rollicking Legion Follies after World War II. *Left to right, top row*: Clifford Fereira, Walter Xavier, Lee Fereira, Ken Witte, Joe Ramos, unidentified, Murph Ramos, Manuel Medina, and Pinky Camacho. *Left to right, bottom row*: Ernie Rose, Brent Bradly, and Merle Johnson. *Museum of the San Ramon Valley.*

south of town. Rex Ide placed a sign on the chair Presley had used and kept patrons from siting in it.

For several years, the American Legion Follies played at the Legion Hall on Hartz and Prospect Avenues. Produced by Legion members, in the follies men dressed in drag and sang, danced, and played instruments to raise funds for veterans. Joe Ramos was "mistress of ceremonies" for the 1949 follies. It was a don't-miss, hilarious event for the entire valley.

201 Front Street

In 1951, a youth center began providing activities, with civic-minded Betty Engelhart as the driving force. Volunteers raised funds for tennis courts to be built at the high school and bought the twenty-year-old Presbyterian church building at 201 Front Street. Staff members were hired to provide activities during the summer.

At a 1989 dedication of the renovated Town Meeting Hall, which was placed in this fifty-year-old building, several people offered stories about the use of the structure.

Wilson Close said that, after a fire, "the second Presbyterian church cost $6,000 and opened in 1933. It was used until 1950, when the congregation outgrew the building. Presbyterian church members bought five acres on El Pintado Road. The new church was completed in December of 1951."

Danville's first police chief, Ken Sandy, recalled that, as a high school student, he worked at the youth center. "I was hired to hand out badminton equipment, volleyballs, pool cues, and things like that for thirty-five cents an hour. So, here I am in the same building making a dollar an hour."

When the center closed, Mrs. Engelhart offered the building to a program for developmentally delayed children. Elree Langford, who was a parent and teacher there, recalled the Lynn Day School, which operated from 1955 to 1984:

> *During the summer of 1955, parents scrubbed, painted and fixed the building, making it ready for a school. In September an open house was held.... The following Monday the doors of the sparkling new school were opened to thirteen mentally retarded preschoolers.... The teacher was Lynn Scarlsboro. The school was named for her.*

The building at 201 Front Street was home to the Lynn Center for the next twenty-nine years. Local merchants and others supported the school. One very special group from Danville continues to support the Lynn Center, the Grandmother Go-Getters Club of Danville.

With the growth of new homes, students came streaming into the schools. Danville Union School District supervisor Ivan Chappell said that in 1951, school attendance increased 304 percent, from 127 to 503. He pointed out that this growth "reflects new residents moving into the county and increasing birth rate." That December, the *Valley Pioneer* reported that two new elementary schools should be ready for the fall of 1952 at a cost (for both) of $477,000.

Many articles in the *Pioneer* reported on civil defense activities. The paper announced that Danville was divided into eleven zones to "function semi-independently in event of a regional emergency."

The largest fire the "SRV had ever known to residents" according to the *Valley Pioneer* demolished the Danville Warehouse and Lumber warehouses on Railroad Avenue in 1952. And the fire district began to move beyond being all-volunteer when Mike Blodgett became a paid fire fighter in 1958. He was fire chief from 1965 to 1988, a challenging time of Danville growth.

Fay Tarlock described one reason people moved to the valley: "In the spring, when the floor of the valley is golden with mustard and the budding walnut trees look like lace from the green hills above, the land is as lovely to newcomers as it was to the Argonauts of old."

Danville reflected the state as a whole in the 1950s: young families growing up and crowding schools, jobs available throughout California, minorities prevented from buying homes, the birth control pill still in the future, and shared values the rule.

14

THE SIXTIES

The 1960s were turbulent years in the country and in Danville. Roiling the culture were the Vietnam War, a new birth control pill, President John F. Kennedy and Dr. Martin Luther King Jr.'s assassinations, a dramatic moon landing, and counterculture events in nearby San Francisco. Locally, many students were out of control with drugs and vandalism and, in 1964, a horrendous plane crash occurred in Tassajara Valley.

The valley changed rapidly as homes replaced ranches; recreation and police services were stretched, and schools needed double sessions. Danville's population was just 3,585 in 1960; it then grew to 9,775 in 1965 (postmaster's estimate) and 16,218 in 1970.

State Route 21 was the major arterial road in place from 1935 to 1967. Traffic along Highway 21 through the valley became unmitigated hell at rush hour, as bumper-to-bumper drivers refused to let people get out of their driveways and side streets. As the new interstate highway was planned and property purchased, everyone agreed it would be totally welcome.

Anyone living in the valley at the time recalled the 1964 Pacific Air Lines plane crash in the Tassajara Valley. A distraught passenger went into the cockpit and shot both pilots. The crash was horrific, with forty-four passengers killed and body parts scattered across the hillsides west of Tassajara Road. Gordon Rasmussen was first on the scene and never wanted to talk about it. *Valley Pioneer* editor Bill Ketsdever said he wouldn't have gone there had he known what he'd find. At the San Ramon Valley Chapel mortuary on Front Street, Mel Whalen and others worked fifty hours straight to take care of the remains.

The San Damiano Retreat, near Las Trampas Wilderness, opened in 1961 and provides a hospitable space for spiritual renewal. *Museum of the San Ramon Valley.*

When Contra Costa County annexed to the East Bay Regional Park District in 1964, the possibility of a large park on Las Trampas Ridge was discussed. Danville's Manfred Lindner and Patrick Whittle formed the Las Trampas Wilderness Committee, which supported the annexation vote, led hikes in the hills, and advocated for a park. By the next decade, the new park covered three thousand acres.

THE FREEWAY CHANGED EVERYTHING

There were plenty of challenges as freeway alignment arguments rang across Danville. Where should it go? Where did the name El Cerro come from? The proposed Diablo Road off-ramp would destroy several old oaks and walnut trees, and irate citizens threatened a boycott of Danville merchants who supported the ramp. The handsome old Flournoy house was also demolished at the off-ramp. *Valley Pioneer* reporters could barely keep up with all the debates.

The new I-680 Freeway segment opened from Walnut Creek to Danville's Sycamore Valley Road on November 11, 1964. An opening celebration was called "Frontier I680" and featured a ribbon-cutting, parade, and lunch. People cheered the prospect of less traffic on the county road.

But what changes the freeway wrought. John May lived on Danville Boulevard and commented that "Danville was in the boonies until the freeway came. It took away the whole 'boonies' aura. Things changed almost overnight." He also said that after the freeway opened, "I went to pick up my papers, and no one was on the boulevard. I came in the house and told my wife things were really eerie out there, like somebody dropped an atom bomb."

Highway 21 signs were taken down as I-680 opened to free-flowing traffic. The first traffic signal in town was placed at the intersection of Hartz Avenue and Diablo Road in May 1972, leading some to think it was the beginning of the end and others to salute progress.

This ribbon was worn to celebrate the I-680 Freeway opening to Sycamore Valley Road in 1964. *Museum of the San Ramon Valley.*

New Homes

Weekly, the *Valley Pioneer* covered growth impacts in the 1960s. Orchards disappeared as homes were built in one area after another, many with walnut or pear trees in their yard. Cameo Acres, Montair, and San Ramon Heights were only a few of the new subdivisions.

One of the valley's first homeowners' groups was formed in Diablo Acres, which developed in the 1950s across from the new Grange Hall on Diablo Road. The Green Valley Neighbors organized because owners were "having troubles with the builder." The group advocated for a variety of improvements and lasted for decades. Called the Green Valley Association by 1977, they also protested County Flood Control's plans for detention ponds in the Green Valley Creek watershed.

A new planned unit development (PUD) zoning designation was adopted by the county in 1964, which permitted smaller lots, green belts and community facilities. Sycamore Homes was the first PUD approved; it had

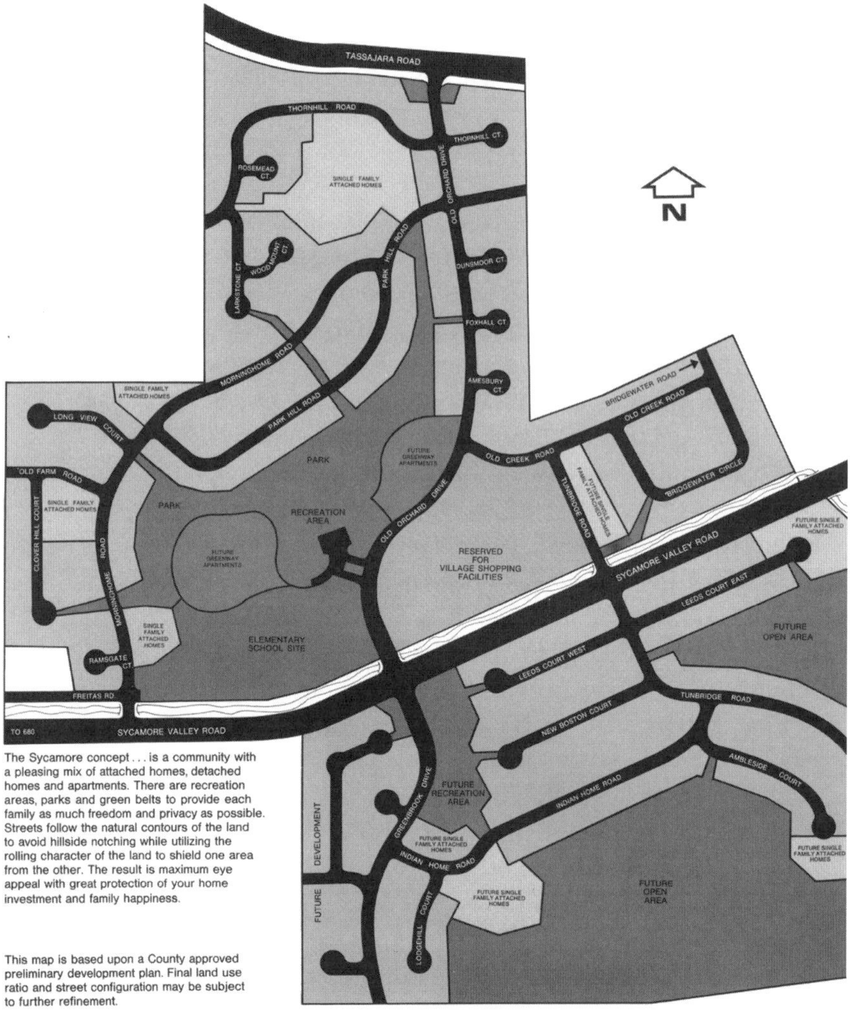

A plan for the first planned unit development Sycamore Homes. It provided shared open spaces and many resident-serving amenities. *Museum of the San Ramon Valley.*

shared open spaces, two pools, tennis courts, and two community buildings. The Greenbrook Homes PUD was approved as well; it covered the historic Meese Ranch and framed San Ramon Creek. Glenview's PUD was planned in the 1960s and provided shared community facilities.

At the same time, taxes for ranches went sky high. Margaret Baldwin Wildenradt said the Osage Ranch taxes increased from \$4,000 to \$44,000 in one year. In 1972, they sold to Kauffman and Broad, which created Danville Station on property that had belonged to the Baldwin family since 1852.

In 1965, the Danville Homeowners Inc. was chartered "to preserve the semi-rural residential character" of the area. They were especially concerned about the new PUD designation. Dick Victor and Manfred Lindner sent a membership appeal, which warned:

> *JUST TWO DEVELOPMENTS CURRENTLY PLANNED FOR THE NEW FUTURE IN DANVILLE WILL INCREASE OUR LOCAL POPULATION BY NEARLY FIFTY PERCENT! AND THAT IS JUST THE BEGINNING.*

The group asserted that whether these changes were high-quality depended on the people. Meanwhile, a Community Planning Committee from the chamber of commerce actively reviewed development plans; these meetings were well attended.

In a *Valley Pioneer* column in 1967, Wilson Close welcomed the new Sycamore Homes, saying, "There just isn't any question that this development will be a great asset to the San Ramon Valley."

New residents often objected to pesticide use nearby. Responding to these complaints, farmers began "to abandon parts, or all, of orchards and fields near houses. This practice left a stock of pests to reinfest the crop and contributed to the willingness of farmers to sell their property for other uses," according to Don Wood.

Schools and Angst

School attendance skyrocketed, with classrooms placed in the Grange Hall, the Methodist church, and St. Isidore Catholic Church in the early 1960s. The only valley-wide elected body was the school board. There were changes afoot.

A ballot measure to unify the various school districts came to the voters in 1964. With state incentives on the line if they unified, after much debate, voters approved the union. They created the San Ramon Valley Unified School District by a vote of 4,330 to 2,617, unifying the six grammar school and one high school district.

The debates didn't stop when a new school board was elected in 1965 and hired innovative thinker Dr. Richard Foster as superintendent instead of the well-respected high school district Superintendent Dr. Roger Schulte. Foster promoted progressive education, built open-space schools, and generally shook things up. Lois Sizoo recalled attending large school board meetings in the school gym and hoping her husband, Wes, wouldn't be shot.

Virginia Deaton helped found the 1962 July Fourth family-friendly celebration and served as a conservative voice on the school board. *Museum of the San Ramon Valley.*

Two years later, the school board election disputes centered on traditional versus liberal education. Wes Sizoo and T. James Athern were replaced by more conservative members Virginia Deaton and William Morison, who opposed "self-directed, self-disciplined techniques" and wanted to instill "systematic teaching of subject matter in an orderly, disciplined manner." The election vote was: Morison, 2,584; Deaton, 2,464; Ahern, 2,247; and Sizoo, 2,131. In 1969, Foster resigned and that April a new superintendent, Dr. Warren Linville, was appointed.

High school students tried drugs, skipped school, traveled to San Francisco for the Summer of Love, and scared everyone during periodic vandalizing sprees. Fosters Freeze was called the drug-dealing center of the valley.

In 1967, about one hundred teenagers attacked cars and people in what the sheriff's office called "One Hell of a Halloween." They threw pieces of concrete, rocks, and eggs at police cars and buildings in Diablo. Then in downtown Danville, they pelted cars from rooftops and on the street. The *Valley Pioneer* reported that editor Doris Rusk "was confronted by 50 teenagers who threw eggs, tomatoes and rocks at her car and tore off the chrome striping on the vehicle. When she got out of her car to take a picture and talk to the teenagers, many of whom she knew, Mrs. Rusk was barraged with rocks and eggs."

Many in the community believed these episodes happened in part because of the shortage of positive youth activities. Danville Bowl opened in the 1960s, offering one new diversion, and the Village Theater provided movies. The Discovery Center for Counseling and Crisis Intervention began in 1971.

Eventually, the school board agreed to hire counselors. Public-minded parents created a new Community Center, which was placed vacant Danville

Elementary School building next to the high school campus. Headed by Dave Stegman, the center provided a variety of programs for youth and initiated a new Senior Citizen Club in 1971. One staffer invited grandmothers to sit at the Fosters Freeze to talk with the youth.

Danville's Downtown

In the 1960s, the commercial section of Danville changed, as original Hartz Avenue businesses closed. At the center of town, at Prospect and Hartz Avenues, Root's Bar and Restaurant (southwest corner) closed after twenty years, as did Acree's Market (northwest corner). The brick bank building on the northeast corner was demolished in 1959. Near the historic Danville Hotel, Russel Glenn constructed the Silver Dollar Room, a restaurant. A new Safeway was established south of Hartz Avenue, and other commercial buildings replaced orchards and homes around the new Sycamore Valley Road freeway access.

General practitioner Dr. John Blemer was an eccentric and competent presence for decades in his office downtown. He provided high school sport

Rancher Hap Magee showing his longhorn cattle in the Silver Dollar Room parking lot near the Danville Hotel, circa 1967. *Museum of the San Ramon Valley.*

physicals, never missed a football game, and was known to read X-rays on the Diablo golf course in his later years.

As the population grew, demands on the post office increased. After outgrowing two offices on East Prospect Avenue, the post office moved to Danville Square in 1966, where it stayed even when another large post office was built east of town on Camino Tassajara twenty years later.

Danville's first three-story building was constructed in 1964 at a cost of $250,000 and was featured in a full section of the *Valley Pioneer* titled "A Salute to Progress." Vern Ryan was the builder. The new Danreco building encompassed sixteen thousand square feet, had wall-to-wall carpets, air conditioning, the first elevator in the valley, and parking available for forty automobiles. It was called "elegant" and "fabulous" in the *Pioneer*.

A *Pioneer* writer explained the predominant opinion:

> *The transition from farmland to residential and commercial has been in effect for a little over a decade, and every few years a development of particular significance reminds us of this growth. The advent of supermarkets in the valley was one such signpost, and the locating of the large commercial firms in San Ramon was another. Now along comes Danville's first three story office building, and the construction of this new edifice has to be classified as one of the vital links in our community's steady progress.*

While some longtime residents were upset about the area's growth, many ranchers became wealthy from the sales of their property. Wilson Close was president of the Danville Renewal Corporation which reviewed a proposed new San Ramon Valley general plan in 1965. One part of the plan recommended extending Diablo Road through the Bank of America parking lot to connect with Railroad Avenue.

The Vietnam War churned American life during the 1960s and '70s, nationally and locally. Danville's first fatality in the war was young Tom Gompertz, an impressive young man who was greatly mourned by his parents and friends. He died in 1968, one month before he was scheduled to return home to study for his doctorate in world economics.

Danville's main street looked scruffy and received some unwanted publicity. The *Pioneer*, on July 3, 1968, reported on one critical article:

> *The Valley's image, already dented by a recently-obtained reputation for having the highest incidence of juvenile delinquency in the County, plus*

Danville's downtown had utility poles and wires, which one newspaper described as a "jungle of signs." The same paper labeled the town "ugly" in 1968. *Museum of the San Ramon Valley.*

> *recent notoriety on the school controversy, took a turn for the worse last month, this time in the field of community appearance....*
>
> *[W]ord comes via the* New Haven Register, *a daily paper of some repute, that California is indeed going to the dogs, beauty-wise, and a six-column photograph, used to depict a typical community in the "Golden State," shows a photo of Hartz Avenue in Danville, with a cutline that reads—"Jungle of signs overrun Danville, California city street."*

Danville Homeowners Inc. was not the first group to address the town's rapid change. There was active criticism of plans approved by the County Planning Commission and supervisors, which resulted in several attempts at incorporation. An Alamo-Danville vote in 1962 lost 2,086 to 1,958. In 1967, a valley-wide incorporation vote went down in flames, 2,796 to 1,958. In the 1970s two more San Ramon Valley cityhood votes were also defeated in 1973 and 1976. It was not until Danville incorporated in 1982 that local control went into effect.

15

A NEW EDGE CITY

1970–2000

Life was changing quickly in the San Ramon Valley, as the area transformed into one of the San Francisco Bay Area's edge cities. A *San Francisco Chronicle* series described the county as an urbanizing "ContraCostapolis." Danville's population grew from 16,218 in 1970 to 19,433 in 1975, with planning, parks, police, and public works managed by Contra Costa County. By 1980, the population was 26,447.

The new freeway opened opportunities for builders as young buyers looked for affordable homes. The Baldwin and Meese Ranches, founded in 1852, became Danville Station and Greenbrook Homes, and Bartlett Ranch became West Briar Knolls.

The Lively Seventies

Las Trampas Regional Wilderness and Mount Diablo framed Danville with thousands of acres of open spaces. But local parks with sport fields and play structures were another matter.

Joe and Roz Hirsch put an appeal in *The Valley Pioneer* for people to meet who wanted local parks. This sparked the creation of the County Service Area R-7, a citizens advisory committee. On June 4, 1974, valley voters approved a $0.25-per-$100 assessment to buy and develop parks. The first committee was chaired by Jim Cain and included Ron Crane, Frankie Ross, and Carol Rosenblum from Danville.

Las Trampas Regional Wilderness provides open spaces and trails at the western edge of Danville. *Museum of the San Ramon Valley.*

Park advocate Sandy Myers recalled, "We hired a plane and had an aerial map produced. Then we circled the areas where parks might go. The top priorities were Osage Station, Oak Hill, Hap Magee Ranch, Central Park in San Ramon and the Bartlett Ranch on La Gonda." Remarkably, all but the Bartlett Ranch became parks. The first Danville parks were the tiny Front Street Park, followed by Oak Hill on Stone Valley Road.

The Iron Horse Regional Trail began after Southern Pacific's San Ramon Branch Line right-of-way was abandoned in 1978. Councilmembers from the new cities and trail advocates led by Bick Hooper and Patrick Whittle provided the local impetus for the Regional Park District to install and manage the Iron Horse Trail. It opened the first section in 1986 and became a popular linear parkway through Danville; it now extends thirty-four miles.

Modern changes came fast and furious in this decade. A new ambulance was officially added to the Danville Fire District. BART opened in 1972. A thrift shop to support the Discovery Center was opened in 1973. Fast food came to the town in 1976, when Burger King opened near the Charlotte

Top: Old Town Danville, with the utility poles and lines buried underground, 1972. *Museum of the San Ramon Valley.*

Bottom: The Danville Oak with two lanes in 1975. *Photographer, Bill Hockins; Museum of the San Ramon Valley.*

Wood Intermediate School. The ten-acre Livery and Mercantile Center opened in 1982. Addressing ever-present fire dangers, the Danville and San Ramon Fire Districts merged in 1980; Tassajara joined in 1990 and, when the Dougherty Regional Fire Authority joined in 1997, the San Ramon Valley Fire Protection District covered the entire valley.

In 1972, after a major chamber of commerce campaign led by Jim Graham, Danville's downtown improved its looks when utilities were put underground at a cost of $198,000. Utility poles were removed and lines were installed underground, amounting to 1.5 miles of cable, 78 splice boxes, and 23 million feet of wire.

An oak tree east of Old Town became a symbol of the community in the 1970s and is now called the Old Danville Oak. It was once located in the yard of Elizabeth and Austin Root. Lambert Wille, who lived nearby, said, "Nobody gave oak trees much credence in those days. An oak tree was an oak tree."

Then a two-lane road bordered the tree, expanding to four lanes in 1976. That year, the Old Town Guild started a party on Friday night after Thanksgiving to tout the tree's importance. At first, about three hundred people gathered at the Danville Hotel Territory, sang carols, and carried lit candles to the Old Danville Oak, which was hung with lights. High school choral groups sang, and Father Christmas (for seventeen years portrayed by local artist Carmine DeVivi) presided over it all. In later years, thousands thronged to enjoy music on Hartz Avenue, Prospect Avenue, and Diablo Road, which were closed to traffic.

The town has nurtured the tree for decades and even surrounded it with a dark green steel wrap in 2001 in case the ancient tree should split and destroy passing cars. Sons of Oak were planted west of the tree in 1997.

Who's in Charge?

With growth exploding, Danville residents were unhappy with many of the county services and asserted that Danville's taxes were being spent elsewhere. Merchants organized as the Old Town Danville Improvement Association in 1976 and funded a plan themselves to upgrade the heart of the commercial area, suggesting a curved Hartz Avenue to move traffic along.

County planners tried to keep up as a new San Ramon Valley general plan was unveiled in 1976, which preserved the ridgelines. It called for a "rural view of life" and included a new land use category called "country estate." By 1980, many issues were stirring people up: the need for more parking downtown; the will to extend Railroad Avenue to Hartz Avenue; a new, looming, three-story bank on Diablo Road (called "precedent-setting"); a county-approved McDonald's near Sycamore Valley Road; and questions about the future of the Charlotte Wood School site.

In 1978, the Danville Association organized with both homeowner and business members "to encourage orderly planning, conserve the natural beauty of the area and encourage measures for the safety and general well-being of the residents," according to its charter. Association leaders reviewed county development plans and spearheaded another incorporation effort, this time voting only in Danville.

Efforts to incorporate Danville had started in the 1960s. Even though Danville advocates started the process, the county's Local Agency Formation Commission would approve only a valley-wide boundary. Since the commission was charged with preventing the creation of unviable new districts or cities, its executive stubbornly insisted on boundaries covering the San Ramon Valley or no vote at all.

Finally, the Danville Association and other advocates convinced the commissioners to allow a Danville-only vote. The proposed town boundaries extended to Crow Canyon Road (with some exceptions) into an area with a San Ramon zip code. Dick McNeely from the Incorporate Danville Committee negotiated with property owners at Danville's edges to establish the lines.

An election on June 8, 1982, created the new Town of Danville. The vote was 5,725 to 4,850, a majority even without the areas with a San Ramon zip code. By that time, the population was 26,447.

The first town council included John May, Beverly Lane, Susanna Schlendorf, Dick McNeely, and Doug Offenhartz. Top vote-getter John May was elected mayor. It was a compatible group, even though their backgrounds were quite divergent. But they all wanted to preserve the Old Town and hillsides, support new buildings in a traditional style, and approve a tight budget.

The town was officially established on July 1, 1982, which was a remarkable achievement since the election had occurred only three weeks earlier. The first town manager was the amiable George Gaekle, who guided the new council to adopt the initial ordinances, hired the first staff, and helped select the next manager, Mike Davis. The Incorporate Danville Committee had used an oak tree logo drawn by Howard Fites of Stuart

Top: A bumper strip with the Danville logo used in Danville's "Yes on B" incorporation campaign. *Museum of the San Ramon Valley.*

Bottom: The new town council was sworn in on July 1, 1982. *Left to right*: John May, Beverly Lane, Dick McNeely, Susanna Schlendorf, and Doug Offenhartz. Judge Max Wilcox Jr. officiated. *Museum of the San Ramon Valley.*

Graphics, and at the July 1 meeting, Stuart Graphics' owner Dick Eastman presented the logo to the town.

The education center at 699 Old Orchard Drive served as the council meeting location from 1982 to 1989. Requests for stop signs, street closures, more parks, better road maintenance, and more police flowed into the council at this location, which was handy for constituents.

The 1980s were a period of intense activity. Mayor John May attended the county mayors conference and weighed in on regional issues, the town joined the Central Contra County Transit Authority for bus service in 1984, and a committee was set up to recommend a new cable company. Initially, the council acted as a planning commission. Whether to hire a Danville staff or become a "contract city" was debated.

A Sycamore Valley specific plan was adopted in 1985, reflecting lengthy county–Danville Association discussions; the plan was completed by a young Danville planner, Joe Calabrigo. In the plan, 2,500 acres were planned for 1,800 homes, saving the hills, planning a trail by Sycamore Creek, and setting up an assessment district. Some of the hills later became the Sycamore Valley Regional Open Space Preserve.

Longtime civic organizations continued their activities, including the Danville Lions Club (1940), the Danville Rotary (1954), the San Ramon Valley Kiwanis (1956), the Alamo-Danville Soroptimists International (1963), the Alamo-Danville Branch of the Association of University Women (1969), and the Danville Association (1978). Later, the Danville–Sycamore Valley Rotary (1989) and San Ramon Valley Rotary (1994) expanded club coverage.

In 1986, the town created a Community Development Agency (Redevelopment Agency), which enabled major improvements, such as the Railroad Avenue parking lot and the extension of Railroad Avenue to Hartz Avenue. A downtown master plan was adopted by the council in 1986 with this goal: "The preservation of the small-scale village character of downtown's buildings and streets."

After the first town general plan was adopted in 1987, appointed commissions helped carry it out. A Planning Commission (started in late 1982) led the way, and a new design review board went to work. Member Gary Vilhauer said that "strict architectural guidelines downtown are a necessary evil because the town is in a critical period of transition." The board advised the commission and council about acceptable architecture and materials, which would reflect the "Danville look." A unique Jiffy Lube design not far from Old Town was offered to other communities as a "Danville design" option.

A Parks and Leisure Services Commission was formed in 1986, which included experienced R-7 committee members Sandy Myers and Ron Crane. They wanted unique parks, each with its own character. Osage

Top: A brick sculpture representing the Camp Swain orphans at Hap Magee Ranch Park. *Artist, Rich Corrin; Museum of the San Ramon Valley.*

Bottom: The historic Eddy house on Hartz Avenue was nearly demolished in 1996. *Photographer, Jim Dotson; Museum of the San Ramon Valley.*

Station had been planned by R-7 and was dedicated in 1988 in the former Osage Ranch pear orchard. In 1989, a ground-breaking trails plan was adopted.

Other commissions, which not all cities created, were set up. In 1990, the council appointed an Arts Commission to support the arts. Danville Area Cultural Alliance (DACA) was created by volunteers and worked with the existing Alamo Danville Artists' Society. Volunteers initiated three Front Street Art Festivals and an art gallery upstairs at the Village Theatre.

A Heritage Resource Commission (HRC) was established in 1988, reflecting a concern for preserving historic buildings. The HRC was designed to encourage owners to keep and renovate these buildings, which was not an easy process. One kerfuffle occurred when Bridges Restaurant wanted to spread its offices and offerings into the historic Eddy house. Because of dry rot and other issues, the building was mostly torn down, retaining only the façade on Hartz Avenue. Councilmembers threw a fit.

While the council listened and sometimes agreed with requests, people got upset when they didn't get their way. The first town office was placed in supervisor Robert Schroder's conference room on Diablo Road; the second was located in an office at 542 San Ramon Valley Boulevard. The expanding staff began bumping into one another. When the council decided to purchase a twelve-year old building for offices at 510 La Gonda Way, citizens objected. An advisory vote opposing the purchase of the building failed in a vote of 4,156 to 3,711 on March 4, 1985.

MYRIAD CONTROVERSIES AND DEBATES

COSTCO CAME CALLING

Citing the need for more income at the urging of John May and Dick McNeely, a big-box warehouse use along the town's southern border was approved by the Planning Commission and council in 1988. There were plenty of objections to such a business, with opponents saying a big-box warehouse did not reflect Danville's small-town atmosphere.

When Costco began looking for a San Ramon Valley location, it first talked to San Ramon. But that city needed eighteen months to change its general plan. The Costco developers decided to move to Danville, which already had the zoning in place. This business is now an important and stable part the town's sales tax income.

The town had its share of other controversies, including a mayor's resignation when he embezzled from his law practice, the dismissal of a manager for alcohol-fueled conduct, a quirky (and unsuccessful) recall of two councilmembers, and a vote to extend Camino Ramon to Fostoria Way near Costco.

Road extensions always brought on hullabaloos. The Railroad Avenue extension, which replaced Linda Lane and displaced the well-regarded San Ramon Valley Lumber Co., connected to Hartz Avenue in 1988. People missed the sweet old intersection of Love Lane and Hartz Avenue. But the opening enabled closures of Hartz Avenue for street fairs and car shows, as well as the Old Danville Oak Tree lightings.

Another storm came with the extension of El Cerro Boulevard to Danville Boulevard, as it was opposed by the Garden Creek Condominium homeowners. Nevertheless, El Cerro Boulevard opened in 1991, with some handsome brick embellishments on the bridge.

The Sycamore Park and Ride was completed in 1996, again with neighborhood objections. Twenty years later, it was difficult to find a space as buses picked up passengers, bikers parked there, and carpools used the lot.

The largest valley development proposed in the 1970s was Blackhawk Homes, in which developer Ken Behring applied for a rezoning on five thousand acres south of Mount Diablo and proposed 4,600 homes. Since the area east of Danville and San Ramon was composed entirely of ranches and ranchettes in 1974, charges of leap-frog development and Mount Diablo foothills destruction came from several sources. Eventually 2,400 homes, clubhouses, and golf courses were constructed, with two thousand acres of open space deeded to Mount Diablo State Park.

Restored Civic Buildings with Some Celebrations

Danville's original county road was Front Street, and actions by the council consistently focused on a core part of Front Street, which had several historic buildings. The 1866 Cohen/Vecki Italianate Gothic house at 169 Front Street was saved and moved closer to the street in 2001. The sixty-year-old Village Theatre was purchased from the Zion Fellowship Gathering Place and restored by the town beginning in 1988. The Role Players Ensemble was started in 1983 to provide live local performances and, in 1991, moved to the Village Theatre.

Adjacent to the theater, today's Town Meeting Hall at 201 Front Street was purchased and rehabilitated as Danville's main meeting space in 1989. In the past, it was used as a Presbyterian church, built in 1933; the Lynn Day School for special needs children from 1955 to 1984; and a Sunday school for the Zion Fellowship's Gathering Place.

In a 1989 dedication of the hall, one speaker was Elaine Collins, coordinator of children's ministries for Zion Fellowship. The building was a Sunday school from 1984 to 1988.

> *I have very fond memories of this building…For hundreds of us that are parents of children who made use of this facility, we have a very warm place in our hearts for it. I can hear little voices ringing out and songs being sung as the children came each Sunday morning to learn God loved them and cared about each one of them.*

At Railroad Avenue, the town also agreed to save the 1891 Danville Depot, providing land for the building and deeding it to the Museum of the San Ramon Valley for a nominal sum. The depot was moved in 1996, restored and opened as a valley history museum and gathering place in 1999.

In 1986, planning began to redevelop the aging ten-acre Charlotte Wood Intermediate School site, setting off a decade-long discussion about financing and use of the site. George Swallow, a local architect, proposed culverting San Ramon Creek and increasing the property's size to twelve acres to expand both public and retail uses. Everyone wanted to keep the former Little League field as an open space.

The town purchased the property in 1993. And in 1996, the seventeen-thousand-square-foot Danville Library, an impressive Community Center, and the Danville Green were dedicated at Front Street and San Ramon Creek. The Danville Green bandstand was donated by the Danville Rotary.

After Monte Vista High School opened in 1965, a rivalry with San Ramon Valley High School began. Their football games had the same local interest as the Stanford–Cal Berkeley Big Game. One Little League All-Star team became national champions in 1978. The sport of soccer eventually took off in popularity. In 1990, the San Ramon Valley High School girls' basketball team won the state championship, the first time any East Bay Athletic League high school team had reached that level of success.

The Danville Library appeared on the Danville Green, near San Ramon Creek. *Town of Danville.*

Women were now in the work force and in elective office, which made some men uncomfortable. In 1986, the San Ramon Valley Kiwanis Club unanimously admitted Joan August to the all-male service club, thought to be the first woman admitted in Northern California. At that point, the international organization had not yet approved of admitting women.

The *Danville Grange Herald*, in 1989, wrote an article with this title: "Survey Says Women Are Running Danville." Polling by George Manross of Survey Research Institute showed women taking the lead in community activities. The council at that point had four women members, which Manross called an "abnormality." He said, "You would like to think that the people who surface in leadership positions would be a representative sample." Mayor Susanna Schlendorf replied, "I don't think it's any more noteworthy than if there were a majority of men running the community."

After years of effort and a lawsuit over access, on May 17, 1985, the new Eugene O'Neill National Historic Site and O'Neill Foundation had a Sunday supper at Tao House, hosted by actress Helen Hayes and funded by Pacific Telesis. A court settlement with Kuss Road neighbors meant limits and restrictions, but the site was a reality. Regular tours of the house and site, plays in the O'Neills' barn, student programs, and other events began in 1995.

By 2000, the town had been incorporated for nearly twenty years. The "Danville Look" throughout Old Town and in properties annexed to the east was a goal the council carried into the next century. By then, the town had a population of 41,715, which remained stable during the next decades.

16

THE TWENTY-FIRST CENTURY

New Year's Eve parties had an unusual vibe with the anticipated arrival of the twenty-first century. The event was titled Y2K, and digital crashes were anticipated everywhere. Would computers work? What about clocks and bank records and Social Security records? Did the lunar spectacle in December portend anything?

The moon appeared 14 percent larger than usual on December 22, 1999, with an impressive newspaper photograph showing it hovering over the Oakland Hills. Alarmists said the monster moon foretold the start of disastrous events. This unusual full moon appeared for the first time in 133 years as the winter solstice and the lunar perigee (the point at which the moon is nearest the Earth) converged.

Danville was no different from any other place in the country when January 1, 2000 arrived without incident. One group of friends celebrated in tuxes at the new Museum of the San Ramon Valley in Danville, toasting the new millennium unscathed.

The first decades of the new century witnessed major growth in Danville's neighboring city, San Ramon, as the Dougherty Valley developed. By 2020, San Ramon had 83,168 residents. Danville was stable in comparison, with 41,715 in 2000, 42,067 in 2010, and 43,559 in 2020.

There were plenty of challenges, as the town's income was modest, residents increasingly resisted density increases, and the COVID pandemic brought virtual meetings and restaurant crises. State housing expectations threatened the character of the town, and technological innovations tested everyone.

Multiple plans and policies guided the town's direction. Some of these included three general plans for 2005, 2010, and 2020; a downtown master plan updated in 2022; a park, recreation and arts strategic plan updated in 2017; and a bicycle master plan adopted in 2021.

ALWAYS THE OLD DANVILLE OAK

When a ferocious storm felled several of the large branches on the Danville Oak, more evaluations of the three-hundred-year-old tree were made. No one wanted to take the treasured tree down; other oaks were planted to the west and anointed as "Sons of Oak." The town council decided to build a steel support structure around the tree to help stabilize it. Doomsday predictions said the tree would totter any moment. In 2001, the structure went up, and now, twenty-five years later, the tree still hasn't fallen.

After thirty-eight years in the 510 La Gonda Way town office building, the town offices moved just south to 500 La Gonda Way in 2022. There were thirty sworn officers for the 18,128-square-mile city, and staff numbers increased only modestly as jobs changed to reflect new technology and better public communication.

Left: The Old Danville Oak lit for the November holiday event. *Danville Area Chamber of Commerce.*

Opposite: The front of the town offices at 500 La Gonda Avenue, with an artist-designed heart. *Photographer, Joe Calabrigo.*

The town council paid tribute to the community's historic identity as they insisted on keeping building heights to two stories (with occasional fudging), facilitating the preservation of some historic buildings, and holding fast to high design standards. When initial plans for the Oak Hill Community Center didn't meet the standards, the town dismissed the architect and settled on local architect Bill Wood to achieve the "Danville Look."

PARTNERSHIPS

With Town Manager Joe Calabrigo's guidance and council approvals, the town budgeted carefully and stretched services with large volunteer programs. The town's lighting and landscape districts helped support streetlights, parks, and roadside and median landscapes; in 2025, voters agreed to increase these funds. People always appreciated periodic street-sweeping. After four decades, the town's budgets continue to focus on police, public works, parks, and planning.

The town collaborated with other government agencies and local organizations to improve school fields and facilities and provide grants to support a vital Old Town. A County Family Justice Center for South County was located in Danville. Major partners include the Eugene O'Neill Foundation, Tao House, the Museum of the San Ramon Valley as Danville's information center, and the Veterans Memorial Building with its veteran services and senior center.

The restoration of the Veterans Memorial Building in the center of Old Town was a major partner-driven accomplishment. It was called the American Legion Hall in 1925. As the hall aged, there were proposals to demolish it and use the property sale to build a more modern hall, as Walnut Creek and Lafayette had done. Veterans and councilmembers debated the hall's future at morning coffee klatches and meetings.

The council purchased the hall from the county, hired Architectural Resources Group of San Francisco for the design, and financed a restored building (from many sources) at a cost of $8.5 million. It opened in April 2012 to great fanfare. The original two-story building continues to be a center for veterans' activities and services. A large auditorium serves many public functions, and offices and meeting rooms became Danville's Senior Center. The total size of the building doubled, from 6,300 to 12,792 square feet.

Known for recognizing the service of veterans, the town supports Armistice Day weekend programs and military features in July Fourth parades. An All Wars Memorial at Oak Hill Park provides remembrances of lives lost in wars. The annual 9/11 commemoration honors the fatalities from the terrorist attack on New York's Trade Centers on September 11, 2001.

Just a block west of the Veterans Memorial Building the Museum of the San Ramon Valley opened in 1999 on town property, providing a gathering place at the corner of West Prospect Avenue and Railroad Avenue. The museum sponsors history programs, an information center, and changing

The 2024 council presented Joe Calabrigo with the Danville Award. *Left to right*: Newell Arnerich, Renee Morgan, Joe Calabrigo, Robert Storer, Karen Stepper, and David Fong. *Town of Danville.*

The Veterans Memorial Building at Prospect and Hartz Avenues in 2012. *Veterans Memorial Building staff.*

Every Saturday, Danville's Farmers' Market serves customers just west of the Museum of the San Ramon Valley. It was started in 1990. *Town of Danville.*

exhibits; schoolchildren come with their history passports, and fourth graders learn about the First People of the Valley each September. Nearby are the Saturday Farmers' Market, the Iron Horse Trail, and shuttles to the Eugene O'Neill National Historic Site.

Another partnership facilitates the autumn Eugene O'Neill Festival, which is produced by the O'Neill Foundation and the National Park Service (NPS). It began in 2000 as an effort to expand community knowledge about the Eugene O'Neill National Historic Site. Owned and managed by the NPS, this site is available via a shuttle on the private Kuss Road. A unique commemorative park with panels featuring O'Neill's Danville-written plays was established on Front Street in 2006.

Memorable Events

In 2009, when Danville resident Chesley "Sully" Sullenberger landed his U.S. Airway airplane on the Hudson River in New York with no lives lost, the town celebrated. People came to the Danville Green in front of the library and cheered the creator of the "Miracle on the Hudson." His feat was the talk of the country and put Danville on the map. He became the Grand Marshal of the Rose Parade in 2010 and threw the ceremonial first pitch of the Major League Baseball opening day for the San Francisco Giants.

Regular Danville events include the popular July Fourth parades, street fairs that close Hartz Avenue, the November Old Danville Oak Tree Lighting, movies on the Danville Green, car shows, and safe Halloween

Sully and Lorrie Sullenberger with Mayor Newell Arnerich at a celebration honoring Sully's "Miracle on the Hudson" in 2009. *Newell Arnerich.*

family walks. In Old Town, the museum, councilmembers, and the O'Neill Foundation give history walks, and a self-guided walk is available using a QR code. Twice a year, public Alamo Cemetery tours with reenactors are provided by the Museum of the San Ramon Valley.

PARKS AND THE ARTS

High-quality parks provide unique designs, timely restorations, and water elements. The original Parks and Leisure Services Commission set the standard: no cookie-cutter parks for Danville. By 2025, there were sixteen large and small parks in the town, each with a different character. Visitors love Hap Magee Ranch Parks and its Canine Corral; Sycamore Valley Park, with its bocce courts and sport fields; Osage Station, with its fields and rose gardens; Diablo Vista's ceramic snake, playgrounds and fields; and Oak Hill's pond, which forms a backdrop for a community center and the All Wars Memorial.

The importance of the arts in the community was recognized by town council members from the start. An Arts Commission established by the first council later morphed to become the Parks, Recreation and Arts Commission in 2020. An Arts District was designated by the council to include the area along Front Street south of East Prospect Avenue. Beginning in 2019, there were seasonal art exhibits staged around the downtown area (hearts and painted benches are just two), and pianos are available to play during summer months.

The Village Theatre itself has had several renovations (1988, 2010, 2013) and now hosts films, live performances, music, and programs for all ages. In 2020, the Role Players Ensemble closed after nearly forty years. The second-floor 1989 Village Theatre Art Gallery became an office space in 2010, as the gallery moved to the more accessible first floor. The theatre received a new moniker, VTAG, for Village Theatre and Art Gallery.

OLD TOWN EVOLVES

The Veterans Memorial Building was remodeled in 2012, the Danville Hotel block was redeveloped in 2014, and Prospect Park Plaza was redone in 2025 at the traditional heart of town at Prospect and Hartz Avenues. They give the old village a new look, although many miss the funky 1960s character of the Danville Hotel area. The actual Danville Hotel and McCauley buildings were saved and repurposed, and many downtown buildings are now a century old.

In Old Town, restaurants and other business have expanded to Railroad Avenue. Shops and restaurants at the Livery and Mercantile Center on Sycamore Valley Road and San Ramon Valley Boulevard draw visitors off the freeway to an attractive rustic-looking center. Some miles to the east, a McDonald's was finally approved, again designed in a traditional style.

Parking was addressed to support the Old Town restaurants, and stores and facilitate a lively walking experience. Five municipal parking lots have been created to support the area, including one which demolished the original San Ramon Valley Chapel/Gagen and McCoy Law building south of the Village Theatre in 2019.

In 2022, a downtown master plan update was adopted by the council, the first since 1986. Its top priorities were more community gathering spaces, stronger connections to and through the downtown, enhanced pedestrian

The Danville Hotel complex, built in 2014, has condominiums on its second floor and retail stores and restaurants on its first floor. *Photographer, Jeff Mason; Museum of the San Ramon Valley.*

Danville Friendship City signs next to the Danville Green. *Photographer, Jeff Mason; Museum of the San Ramon Valley.*

safety, and opportunities to support the town's arts and culture. The planned Theatre Plaza between the town meeting hall and Village Theatre was a popular addition. And everyone noticed the new Danville Oak Tree logo placed in the street at Diablo Road and Hartz Avenue.

Always ready for a celebration, in 2008, the town remembered its sesquicentennial with some parties and a coffee table book called *Vintage Danville: 150 Years of Memories*. Spreading its wings a little, Danville now has two Friendship Cities, New Ross, Ireland (2017), and Danville, Kentucky (2021). And Danville was named the safest city for its size in California from 2017 to 2024.

Housing Requirements Bring Challenges

With concerns about sufficient housing, fifty years ago, the state legislature required that cities include a housing element in their general plans. Goals for the numbers of dwelling units in each city were assigned every eight years. In 2016, the state assigned Danville 557 dwelling units, including 140 very low–income and 88 low-income units.

The town complied through its own inclusionary ordinance, which required a certain percentage of affordable units in each new development and enabled more senior housing and higher densities near bus lines. Accessory dwelling units, called "garden cottages," were designed in Craftsman, Mediterranean and Contemporary styles, from which applicants could choose and which shortened the town's permit process.

Then, with homelessness on the rise and a shortage of housing, state agencies increasingly passed bills which assigned larger numbers of new houses to cities. In the 2023 to 2031 cycle, the state quadrupled the number of housing units assigned to Danville to 2,241. The new number was intimidating for a built-out community with 16,551 dwelling units. Census figures indicate that 34.2 percent of the town's population was over the age of fifty-five. And people don't want to move away from Danville.

For a community that prided itself on a certain architectural look and restricted building heights and fought to keep Old Town Danville looking "high touch," the numbers were a shock. How to keep Danville's character and meet the goal was the council's primary discussion.

As more dense housing was approved by the town, critics attacked the changes in Danville. They objected to the large Danville Hotel complex, the Alexan Downtown Danville's 144 apartments at Diablo Road and the freeway, and The Nova's 50 senior apartments south of El Cerro on El Pintado. Faz Restaurant, with its popular tree-lined patio, closed. In 2025, it was replaced by "600 Hartz," with 37 condos on the second floor, retail space, and underground parking. People were unhappy to see the huge redwood trees cleared and criticized the building size.

These debates and home costs were a far cry from the first affordable houses that were built as the freeway was planned in the 1950s; then arguments focused on lot sizes of one-third or one-quarter acre. Some houses in Cameo Acres, Greenbrook, and Montair sell for twenty times their original prices, as the average Danville home value in 2025 rose to $1,995,056.

Contemporary Danville

Danville's reputation as a desirable place to live has popped up in unusual places. Tom Wolfe's book *A Man in Full* has one character who dreams of saving enough money to live "in a condo in Danville…a lovely leafy little town with pretty houses and pretty shops, an oasis." In *Pearls Before Swine*, a popular cartoon by Stephen Pastis, one character begins his book tour in Danville, California.

For over forty years, the town council has worked to preserve the character of Danville's central core and respond to what their voters want and appreciate. It is clear councilmembers like serving and taking turns as mayor. In 2024, the council reflected eighty-three years of experience, with two people serving over twenty years. Town Manager Joe Calabrigo had a long tenure as town manager, serving from 1993 to 2025. During that time, there have been only nineteen councilmembers. The new manager is Tai Williams.

And what of the future? Experts predict that in twenty years, there is a 99 percent chance of a substantial earthquake on the Hayward or Calaveras Faults. Housing issues will continue to roil, with state legislators pushing the boundaries. A new Diablo Road trail is in the works. With its stunning physical environment, goals for a walkable downtown, unique parks, and fiscal stability, Danville attracts people, and they don't want to leave.

Appendix A

PUBLIC SERVICE

Danville Postmasters

The Danville Post Office was established on August 31, 1860, at the Danville Hotel.

Postmaster	Date of Appointment
Henry W. Harris	August 31, 1860
Michael Cohen	July 3, 1865
Henry Hurst	November 23, 1877
Michael Cohen	August 23, 1878
John Conway	May 15, 1886
John A. Shuey	August 21, 1889
John Conway	October 9, 1893
Teresa Conway	September 22, 1896

Postmaster	Date of Appointment
Albert E. Clark	February 24, 1898
Emma Dodge	February 11, 1913
Ruby M. Podva	September 30, 1933
Henry H. Neidenbach	October 31, 1963
La Vern J. Morris	February 6, 1973
Robert B. Dupart	January 26, 1979
Leon T. Pendarvis	May 5, 1979
Albert Reed	July 11, 1981
Albert A. Bowen	March 6, 1982
Ronald J. Elizondo	December 1, 1990
George Cunningham	June 29, 1991
Margaret Muller	October 16, 1999
Cathy Ott	April 22, 2000
Henry A. Richards	October 20, 2008
Janell L. Olsen	November 8, 2008
Romeo S. Deguzman	March 9, 2013
Micelina V. Soriano	March 5, 2016
Jesus R. Avila	April 11, 2020

Danville Fire Chiefs

1912	Joe A. Freitas	Danville Farm Defense Fire District
1922	Oscar Olsson	Danville Fire Protection District
1925	H.M. Fichtenmueller	Danville Fire Protection District
1947	Duane Elliott	Danville Fire Protection District
1961	William Van Limburgh	Danville Fire Protection District
1964	Forrest Wilson	Danville Fire Protection District
1965	Michael W. Blodgett	Danville Fire Protection District

San Ramon Valley Fire Protection District

1980	Michael W. Blodgett
1988	Mel Deardorff
1996	William Dutcher
1999	Rick Probert
2002	Craig Bowen
2008	Richard Price
2013	Paige Meyer

County Supervisors Representing Danville from 1850 to 2025

1852	Samuel H. Robinson, Victor Castro, Robert Farrelly, William Patten, and T.J. Keefer	At Large
1853	Samuel H. Robinson, Cummings Lund, E.D. Winn, William Patten, and T.J. Keefer	At Large
1854	A.W. Genung, Joseph Martin, Carroll W. Ish, Isaac Hunsaker, and J.C. McMaster	At Large
1855	L.L. Morgan and Nathaniel Jones	District 2
1856–1861	Ira J. True	
1862–1864	J.R.L. Smith	
1865–1876	D.N. Sherburne	
1877–1879	Walter Renwick	
1880–1881	D.N. Sherburne	
1882–1885	T.E. Middleton	
1886–1887	J. Kelley	
1888–1892	James M. Stow	
1893–1900	William Hemme	
1901–1904	James. M. Stow	
1905–1908	Ralph Harrison	
1909–1923	J.P. Casey	
1923–1932	Oscar Olsson	

1933–1956	H.L. Cummings
1957–1964	Mel F. Nielsen
1964–1972	James E. Moriarty
1973–1976	Edmund A. Linscheid
1977–1980	Eric Hasseltine
1981–1992	Robert Schroder
1993–1997	Gayle Bishop
1998–2003	Donna Gerber
2003–2004	Millie Greenberg
2005–2011	Mary N. Piepho
2011–2012	Gayle B. Uilkema
2012–present	Candace Andersen

DANVILLE COUNCILMEMBERS 1982–2025

John May
Beverly Lane
Richard McNeely
Susanna Schlendorf
Doug Offenhartz
Richard Kennett
Millie Greenberg
Don Ritchey
Barbara Jagger
Mike Shimansky
Mike Doyle
Dick Waldo
Newell Arnerich
Karen Stepper
Candace Andersen
Robert Storer
Renee Morgan
Lisa Blackwell
David Fong
Mark Belotz

Appendix B

INCORPORATION EFFORTS IN THE SAN RAMON VALLEY WITH DANVILLE VOTES, 1964–1982

Alamo-Danville

September 29, 1964

Lost 2,086 to 1,958

Council would have been T. James Ahern, Herman Sandkuhle, Max Lauritzen, Richard Moulds, and John Hartwell.

San Ramon Valley

December 19, 1967

Lost 2,796 to 1,830

Council would have been Roy Anderson, Byron Athan, Francis Driscoll, George Filice, and John May.

San Ramon Valley

January 23, 1973

Lost 5,623 to 5,178

Council would have been Roy Bloss, Eric Hasseltine, Dick Kennett, Claudia Nemir, and Brian Thiessen.

San Ramon Valley

November 2, 1976

Lost 10,426 to 7,846

Council would have been Claudia Nemir, Bob Bush, Norm Roberts, Gene Rolandelli, and Don Sledge.

Danville

June 2, 1982

Won 5,725 to 4,850

Council became John May, Beverly Lane, Dick McNeely, Susanna Schlendorf, and Doug Offenhartz.

Appendix C

HISTORICAL PLAQUES IN DANVILLE

San Ramon Valley Historical Society Plaques

Alamo Cemetery, 130 El Portal
Albert J. Young house, 911 San Ramon Valley Boulevard
Charles G. Goold family, Redwood Grove in the Sycamore Shopping Center
Cohen-Vecki house, 169 Front Street
Danville Grammar School, southwest of Village Theatre
Danville Grange No. 85, 233 Front Street (second floor of Village Theatre)
Danville Hotel, 411 Hartz Avenue
Danville Southern Pacific Depot, 205 Railroad Avenue
James E. Close family, south side of Diablo Road, across from Rose Street
Mount Diablo, summit
San Ramon Southern Pacific Depot, north of Fostoria Way
San Ramon Valley High School, 501 Danville Boulevard
Spanish 1772 campsite, El Portal and Danville Boulevard
Sycamore Grammar School, near corner of Camino Tassajara and Wood Ranch Road
Tassajara Grammar School, 1650 Finley Road
Tatcan Indians, north of the Danville Green by San Ramon Creek
Union Academy Site, 902 Danville Boulevard
Veterans Memorial Building, 400 Hartz Avenue

Danville Heritage Resource Commission Plaques

Austin Root house, 120 West Linda Mesa Avenue
Bert Read house, 571 Hartz Avenue
Boone-Osborn house, 15 Serena Lane
Bret Harte Park, Diablo Road and Camino Tassajara
Cabral house, 551 Hartz Avenue
Cooley house, 154 East Prospect Avenue
Danville Hotel, 411 Hartz Avenue
Danville's Old Oak Tree, middle of Diablo Road
Eddy house, 500 Hartz Avenue
Fazzio-Fisher house, 342 Railroad Avenue
Fredrickson house, 178 East Prospect Avenue
George and Minnie Foster house, 402 Hartz Avenue
Grange Hall, 233 Front Street
Hap Magee Ranch Park, 1025 La Gonda Way
James Root Sr. house, 90 Railroad Avenue
Joe and Annie Foster house, 404 Hartz Avenue
Love house, 357 Love Lane
McCauley house, 411 Hartz Avenue
McDonald's Drug Store, 345/349 Hartz Avenue
Podva farmhouse, 809 Podva Road
Presbyterian church, 201 Front Street
Rays Pool House/Xavier's Shoe Store, 375 Hartz Avenue
Shuey-Podva house, 100 School Street
Southern Pacific Depot, 205 Railroad Avenue
Tatcan–Bay Miwok, Danville Green and bridge
Vecki house, 169 Front Street
Veterans Memorial Building, 400 Hartz Avenue

Parks with Plaques

Bret Harte Park, Diablo Road and Camino Tassajara
Hap Magee Ranch Park, 1025 La Gonda Way

- Camp Swain plaque, near the Cottage
- Tatcan Indian commemorative plaque, near the small dog park

June Ramos Park, El Pintado, volunteers recognized
Oak Hill Park, All Wars Memorial

O'Neill Park, Front Street, Eugene O'Neill plays
Osage Station Park, 816 Brookside Drive, Baldwin Ranch history

National Register of Historical Places with Plaques

Danville Depot, added to register in 1994
Eugene O'Neill Historic Site, added to register in 1974
Tassajara Grammar School, added to register 2012

Other Plaques

Danville Fire District founding, 356 Hartz Avenue
Gina Lollobrigida pedestrian bridge, from Iron Horse Trail to Danville Square
Reverend R.S. Symington remembrance, on redwood tree, 201 Front Street
St. Isidore Catholic Church, tower on the north side
Veterans' plaques at the Veterans Memorial Building

BIBLIOGRAPHY

A Centennial to Remember

Danville Sentinel. "Danville's Beginnings." January 1898.

Dressen, Rick. "Daniel Inman, Namesake of Danville." Unpublished essay, 1993.

The History of the Danville Hotel and McCauley House. Nearon Enterprises, 2002. Pamphlet.

Richards, Helen. "Danville Withdraws from the Twentieth Century." *Contra Costa Times*, January 26, 1959.

Tarlock, Fay. "Danville—A Portrait." *The Valley Pioneer* (Centennial Edition, 1858–1958), September 4, 1958.

Danville's Setting and First People

Bean, Lowell L. "Indians of California: Diverse and Complex Peoples." *Magazine of the California Historical Society* 71, no. 3 (Fall 1992): 302–23.

Brewer, William H. *Up and Down California in 1860–1864*. University of California Press, 1974.

Butz, Inez. *Danville Notes*. Museum of San Ramon Valley Archives.

Contra Costa Gazette. October 21, 1868.

———. October 24, 1868.

———. October 31, 1868.

———. April 19, 1906.

Crane, Ron, and Kevin Crane. "Geology of the San Ramon Valley: A Personal Account of the Present Geological Knowledge of the Area." Unpublished monograph, 2002.

Edmonston, Vivian Coats. "The Good Old Daze." Contra Costa County Historical Society program. May 14, 1970.

Jones, Virgie V. *Historical Persons & Places…in San Ramon Valley*. Morris-Burt Press, 1977.

Millken, Randall. *Native Americans at Mission San José*. Malki-Ballena Press, 2008.

———. *A Time of Little Choice: The Disintegration of Tribal Culture in the San Francisco Bay Area 1769–1810*. Ballena Press, 1995.

Ortiz, Bev. "Mount Diablo." *News from Native California* (March/April 1988).

———. *The Ohlone Past and Present: Native Americans of the San Francisco Bay*. Edited by Lowell J. Bean. Ballena Press, 1994.

Wood, Charlotte. "Rambling Reminiscences of the Charles Wood Family and Their 'Woodside Farm' Home." Unpublished monograph, 1951.

The Spanish Invasion

Amador, José María. *Land Case No. 287 in the Northern District Court*. 1852. Bancroft Library.

———. *Recollections*. An oral history taken by Thomas Savage in 1877 and translated by Earl R. Hewitt. Bancroft Library.

Bancroft, Hubert H. *History of California*. Vol. 6, 1848–1859. Wallace Hebberd, 1963.

Brewer, William H. *Up and Down California in 1860–1864*. University of California Press, 1966.

Hoover, Mildred, Hero Rencsh and Ethel Rensch. *Historic Spots in California*. Revised by William N. Abeloe. Stanford University Press, 1966

Milliken, Randall. *Native Americans at Mission San José*. Malki-Ballena Press, 2008.

Mount Diablo Summit Native Peoples. State of California exhibit text, 2003.

Sandos, Professor John. Private communication with the author, 2018.

Gold in the Hills and Valley: 1850–1870

Bancroft, Hubert H. *History of California*. Vol. 6, 1848–1859. Wallace Hebberd, 1963.

Contra Costa Gazette. December 24, 1861.

———. January 1, 1864.

———. July 16, 1864.

———. October 8, 1864.

———. October 21, 1864.

———. October 31, 1868.

———. September 17, 1887.

Jones, Virgie V. *Remembering Alamo…and Other Things Along the Way*. Morris-Burt Press, 1975.

Munro-Fraser, J.P. *History of Contra Costa County, California*. W. A. Slocum & Co., 1882.

Smith, James. *Recollections*. Edited by Gary B. Drummond. GRT Book Printing, 1995.

Wood, Charlotte. "Rambling Reminiscences of the Charles Wood Family and Their 'Woodside Farm' Home." Unpublished monograph, 1951.

Creating a Community

Akers, Scott R. "A History of the Grain Industry in Contra Costa County 1859–1910." Master's thesis, San Diego State College, July 1971.

Burgess, Robert Noble. *Memoirs*. Privately published, 1964.

Butz, Inez. "History of the Danville Grange." Unpublished monograph, 1984.

Jones, Virgie V. *Historical Persons & Places…in San Ramon Valley*. Morris-Burt Press, 1977.

Lane, Beverly. *Brief Chronology of Danville Libraries*. Unpublished manuscript, 2013.

Munro-Fraser, J.P. *History of Contra Costa County*. W.A. Slocum Publisher, 1882.

Pacific Rural Press. "A Farm Visit." May 14, 1887.

Smith, James D. *Recollections*. Edited by Gary B. Drummond. GRT Book Printing, 1995.

Smith, Ross W. *History of the Danville Grange*. Ashford Publications, 2007.

Stewart, Will E. "The Danville Grange." Unpublished monograph, n.d.

An Agrarian Century

Alta California. March 8, 1860.

Brewer, William H. *Up and Down California in 1860–1864*. University of California Press, 1966.

Byron Times (Tenth Development Edition, 1926–27).

Contra Costa Gazette. March 26, 1887.

———. April 16, 1887.

———. May 30, 1892.

Cozine, Ralph. "Agriculture: For a Century the Business of the Valley." Unpublished monograph, 2002.

Davis, William Heath. *Seventy-Five Years in California*. John Howell, 1929.

Hall, Lucy. *Danville Rotary Pioneers*. Video. 1982.

Lane, Beverly. "A History of Ranching in the San Ramon Valley." *California Historian* 59, nos. 1–2 (2014): 42–47.

Muir, Joseph. "History of the Cattle Industry in Contra Costa and Alameda Counties." *California Cattleman*, March 1965.

Munro-Fraser, J.P. *History of Contra Costa County, California*. W.A. Slocum Publisher, 1882.

Nash, Gerald D. *Stages of California Economic Growth 1870–1890: An Interpretation*. Ward Richie Press, 1973.

Pacific Rural Press. "Contra Costa County Fair." October 10, 1874.

———. "A Farm Visit." May 14, 1887.

Purcell, Mae Fisher. *History of Contra Costa County*. Gullick Press, 1940.

Rego, Nilda. "Cream Separator Helped Dairy." *Days Gone By*, March 2, 1996.

Rutherford, Richard. "The $$$ Trend, Red and Black, a History of Agriculture in the San Ramon Valley." *Valley Pioneer* (Centennial Edition, 1858–1958), September 4, 1958.

San Ramon Valley Herald. "San Ramon Ranchers Look Back." June 8, 1990.

Smith, James D. *Recollections*. Edited by Gary B. Drummond. GRT Book Printing, 1995.

Tri-Valley News. July 26, 1974.

Wood, Charlotte. "Rambling Reminiscences of the Charle Wood Family and Their 'Woodside Farm' Home." Unpublished monograph, 1951.

Wood, Don. "Random Recollections of Things I've Seen or Been Told." Unpublished monograph about San Ramon Valley agriculture, 2002.

———. *Wood Ranch Buildings: What I Know or Have Been Told*. Compiled by Cynthia Wood Rivera, with photographs from the Wood family archives. Shutterfly, 2021.

Getting Around: Roads and Rails

Bean, Walton, and James Rawls. *California: An Interpretive History* McGraw-Hill, 1983.

Blackmur, Arnold. *In Old Diablo: A Social History*. Ampex Corp., 1981.

Boone, Ruth. Interview with the author. 1990.

Burgess, Robert Noble. *Memoirs*. Privately published, 1964.

Byron Times (Tenth Development Edition, 1926–27). 97–98.

Close, Wilson. Interview with the author. 1976.

Contra Costa Courier and Danville Journal. July 4, 1919.

———. February 29, 1924.

Contra Costa Gazette. September 12, 1891.

———. February 17, 1894.

———. January 6, 1900.

———. Clippings from 1890 and 1891. Collected by Roy Bloss.

Danville Grange Herald. February 24, 1923.

———. July 21, 1923.

———. November 10, 1923.

Danville Sentinel. May 14, 1915.

Demoro, Harre W. *California's Electric Railways, an Illustrated Review*. Interurban Press, 1986.

Dotson, Irma M. *The Danville Branch of the Oakland Antioch & Eastern Railway*. Museum of the San Ramon Valley, 1996.

———. *San Ramon Branch Line of the Southern Pacific*. Museum of the San Ramon Valley, 1991.

Jones, Virgie V. *Historical Persons and Places…in San Ramon Valley*. Morris-Burt Press, 1977.

Lane, Beverly. *Before BART: Electric Railroads Link Contra Costa County*. Contra Costa County Historical Society, 2012.

Mercurio, John, and Steve Minniear. *Highway 21: The Farm Road That Became an Interstate in the San Ramon and Amador Valleys*. Conference of California Historical Societies, October 20–23, 2016.

Ogden, Paul. Interview with Andrew Young. 1987.

San Francisco Chronicle. December 14, 1923.

Swett, Ira L. *Sacramento Northern Through the Sacramento Valley*. Interurban Press, 1962.

Tarlock, Fay. "Danville—A Portrait." *The Valley Pioneer* (Centennial Edition, 1858–1958), September 4, 1958.

Tri Valley News. July 28, 1973.

Walnut Kernel (Tenth Anniversary Edition). 1941.
Wildenradt, Margaret Baldwin. Interview with the author. 1991.
Wood, George. Interview in the *Danville Rotary* video. 1987.

Danville Grows into Its Own: 1870–1900

Contra Costa Gazette. March 26, 1887.
———. February 17, 1894.
———. December 19, 1896.
———. October 8, 1897.
———. February 10, 1900.
Dotson, Irma M. *The San Ramon Branch of the Southern Pacific*. Museum of the San Ramon Valley, 1991.
Dotson, Irma M., and Jim Dotson. *Downtown Danville, 1976–2001: Pictorial Historical and Business Notes*. Irma M. Dotson, 2001.
Lane, Beverly. "Yesteryear in the San Ramon Valley." Unpublished monograph, 2013.
Pacific Rural Press. "A Farm Visit." May 14, 1887.
Purcell, Mae Fisher. *The History of Contra Costa County*. University of California Press, 1950.
Root, Ina Boone. Interview. 1958.
Wood, Charlotte. *History of Danville, Contra Costa County, California*. Danville Women's Club Program, 1946.
———. "Rambling Reminiscences of the Charles Wood Family and Their 'Woodside Farm' Home." Unpublished monograph, 1951.

The Twentieth Century: 1900–1930

Butz, Inez. "The Founding and Early Years of the San Ramon Valley Union High School District." Unpublished monograph, 1984.
Contra Costa Courier and Danville Journal. March 12, 1914.
Contra Costa Gazette. July 12, 1891.
———. February 17, 1894.
———. December 19, 1896.
———. February 10, 1900.
———. August 26, 1911.
———. March 12, 1914.

———. May 6, 1918.
———. May 18, 1918.
———. October 5, 1918.
Deardorff, Mel (chief). "Danville Fire District Minutes." 1991. Speech.
Edmonston, Vivian Coats. "The Good Old Daze." Contra Costa County Historical Society program. May 14, 1970.
Jones, Virgie V. *Historical Persons and Places…in San Ramon Valley*. Morris-Burt Press, 1977.
———. *Remembering Alamo…and Other Things Along the Way*. Morris-Burt Press, 1975.
San Ramon Fire Protection District: 75 Years of Service. San Ramon Valley Fire Protection District, 1987. Booklet.
Tarlock, Fay. "Danville—A Portrait." *Valley Pioneer* (Centennial Edition, 1858–1958), September 4, 1958.
Tatum, Robert D. *Old Times in Contra Costa: A Journey to the Past*. Highland Publishers, 1993.

Let's Party!

Contra Costa Gazette. December 2, 1892.
———. December 2, 1893.
———. May 6, 1918.
Cozine, Marillyn, et. al. *Danville: Portrait of 125 Years*. Town of Danville, 1984.
Danville Grange Herald. October 8, 1951.
Edmonston, Vivian Coats. "The Good Old Daze." Contra Costa County Historical Society program. May 14, 1970.
Hall, Lucy. Interview by Danville Rotary. 1982.
Martinez Daily Gazette. April 18, 1906.
Smith, James D. *Recollections*. Edited by Gary B. Drummond. GRT Book Printing, 1995.
Tarlock, Fay. "Danville—A Portrait." *Valley Pioneer* (Centennial Edition, 1858–1958), September 4, 1958.
Tri-Valley Herald. October 8, 1981.
Tri-Valley News. July 28, 1974.
———. April 12, 1980.
Wiester, Hazel. Interview by Danville Rotary. 1982.

Years of Challenge: 1930–1945

Ajari, Jun. Interview with the author. 1996.
Concord Transcript. January 27, 1938.
Contra Costa Gazette. April 30, 1931.
Ferreira, Rose, and Joe Ferreira. Interview with Arnold Blackmur. 1977.
Handa, Ace. Interview with the author. 1996.
Lane, Beverly. "Yesteryear in the San Ramon Valley." Unpublished monograph, 2013.
Muir, Joseph, and George McNeely. *History of the Cattle Industry in Contra Costa and Alameda County*. California Cattlemen, March 1966.
Tarlock, Fay. "Danville—A Portrait." *Valley Pioneer* (Centennial Edition, 1858–1958), September 4, 1958.
Tri-Valley Herald. October 8, 1981.
Tri-Valley News. January 28, 1976.
———. April 12, 1980.
Valley Pioneer. March 10, 1949.
———. August 9, 1951.
———. December 28, 1951.
———. September 9, 1981.
Vincent, Bob. Interview with the author. 1991.
Wood, Don. Interview with the author. 2011.
Wood, George. Interview in the *Danville Rotary* video. 1984.

Eugene O'Neill in Danville

Chappell, Gordon S. Kenneth Macgowan letters from September 10 and 20, 1937. In *Historical Resources, Eugene O'Neill National Historic Site*. Department of the Interior, 1990.
Clark, Barrett. *Eugene O'Neill: The Man and His Plays*. Dover Publications, 1947.
Cooper, Wendy. *Chronology of Tao House, 1937–2024*. Unpublished monograph, 2024.
———. Interview with the author. 2025.
Cummins, Dorothy, ed. *Love Admiration and Respect: The O'Neill-Commins Correspondence*. Duke University Press, 1986.
Gelb, Arthur, and Barbara Gelb. *O'Neill*. Harper and Row, 1973.
Hornbeck, Hulet. Interview with the author. 2004.

A Village Transformed: 1945–1960

Central Contra Costa Sanitary District. Minutes. September 27, 1954.

Lane, Beverly. Transcription of the Town Hall dedication meeting. December 4, 1989.

———. "Yesteryear in the San Ramon Valley." Unpublished monograph, 2013.

Muir, Joseph. *History of the Cattle Industry in Contra Costa and Alameda County*, California Cattlemen, March 1966.

Root, Viola Scott. "History of Danville." Unpublished monograph, 1972.

Tarlock, Fay. "Danville—A Portrait." *Valley Pioneer* (Centennial Edition, 1858–1958), September 4, 1958.

Valley Pioneer. August 9, 1945.

———. July 7, 1949.

———. November 3, 1949.

———. October 4, 1951.

———. December 28, 1951.

———. November 15, 1952.

———. September 15, 1955.

———. October 29, 1958.

The Sixties

Alamo-Danville Observer. December 10, 1965.

Close, Wilson. "Close-Ups." *Valley Pioneer*, June 28, 1967.

Gonzales, J. Ernest. Review of *How to Kill a Golden State*, by William Bronson. *New Haven Register*, June 16, 1968.

Stegman, Dave. Interview with the author. 2008.

Valley Pioneer. August 17, 1964.

———. April 13, 1965.

———. April 20, 1965.

———. April 19, 1967.

———. November 1, 1967.

———. February 14. 1968.

———. November 20, 1974.

———. August 10, 1977.

———. March 8, 1978.

———. October 8, 1986.

Victor, Dick, and Manny Lindner. *Danville Homeowners, Inc.* Self-published brochure. 1965.

Wildenradt, Margaret Baldwin. Interview with the author. 1991.

Wood, Don. *Wood Ranch Buildings: What I Know or Have Been Told.* Compiled by Cynthia Wood Rivera, with photographs from the Wood family archives. Shutterfly, 2021.

A New Edge City: 1970–2000

Calabrigo, Joe. *Danville Chronology*. Self-published, 2025.

Cooper, Wendy. "A Chronology of Tao House, 1937–2024." Unpublished monograph, 2024.

Lane, Beverly. "Yesteryear in the San Ramon Valley." Unpublished monograph, 2013.

San Francisco Chronicle. January 1984.

San Ramon Valley Herald. May 12, 1989.

———. December 25, 1997.

Tri-Valley Herald. September 4, 1996.

Tri-Valley News. July 28, 1973.

———. September 26, 1976.

Valley Pioneer. July 26, 1967.

———. June 6, 1972.

———. December 11, 1974.

———. April 28, 1976.

———. September 29, 1976.

———. September 14, 1977.

———. October 6, 1986.

———. December 10, 1986.

———. August 31, 1988.

The Twenty-First Century

Arnerich, Newell. Interview with the author. 2025.

Belotz, Mark. Interview with the author. 2025.

Calabrigo, Joe. *Danville Chronology*. Self-published, 2025.

———. Interview with the author. 2025.

Cooper, Wendy. "A Chronology of Tao House, 1937–2024." Unpublished monograph, 2024.

Crompton, David. Interview with the author. 2025.

Fereira, Chuck. Interview with the author. 2025.

Korbmacher, Fred. Interview with the author. 2025.

Morgan, Renee. Interview with the author. 2025.

Pastis, Stephen, "Pearls Before Swine (cartoon)." *Contra Costa Times*, October 1, 2023.

Perezalonso, Henry. Interview with the author. 2025.

San Francisco Chronicle. "Moonshine on the Bay." December 22, 1999.

San Ramon Valley Herald. "Moon Rises to Solstice Occasion." December 23, 1999.

Stepper, Karen. Interview with the author. 2025.

Storer, Robert. Interview with the author. 2025.

Williams, Tai. Interview with the author. 2025.

Wolfe, Tom. *A Man in Full*. Bantam Books, 1998.

INDEX

C

D

E

K

L

M

N

O

P

R

S

Y

Z

ABOUT THE AUTHOR

Beverly Lane is the author of this new book about Danville, California. A graduate of Occidental College in Los Angeles, she is a historian who has written about California and San Ramon Valley history for decades. After pursuing extensive research on local history, she has given lectures and written newspaper columns, monographs, magazine articles and books about the Contra Costa County area. Her writings include *San Ramon Valley: Alamo, Danville, San Ramon*; *San Ramon, Chronicles of Bygone Days*; *Vintage Danville, 150 Years of Memories*; *Historic Tales of Alamo*; and *Before BART: Electric Railroads Link Contra Costa County*. A community organizer and elected official, she has served as the mayor of Danville and president of the East Bay Regional Park District Board. She and her family have lived in Danville for over fifty years.